*Helena*

# *Helena*

## *A Novel*

### *by*

## MACHADO de ASSIS

Translated,

with an introduction,

by

Helen Caldwell

UNIVERSITY OF CALIFORNIA PRESS

Berkeley      Los Angeles      London

University of California Press
Berkeley and Los Angeles, California

University of California Press, Ltd.
London, England

Copyright © 1984 by The Regents of the University of California

Library of Congress Cataloging in Publication Data

Machado de Assis, 1839-1908.
Helena: A Novel.        Translation of: Helena.
I. Caldwell, Helen.      II. Title.
PQ9697.M18H4      1984        869.3        83-17966
ISBN  0-520-04812-1

Printed in the United States of America

1  2  3  4  5  6  7  8  9

*Note: Helena* was published in installments in *O Globo* (Rio), Aug.-Sept., 1876; in book form, October of the same year: *Helena/* por/ Machado de Assis/ Rio de Janeiro / B. L. Garnier/ Livreiro-Editor do Instituto Historico Brasileiro/ 65 Rua do Ouvidor/ 1876.

The text of the present translation is the Jackson edition of 1944, with alternate readings suggested by other editions, in particular: Machado de Assis/ *Helena/ Iaiá* Garcia/ Organização, introdução, revisão de texto e notas/ de/ Massaud Moisés/ Editors Cultrix, São Paulo, 1960; and Machado de Assis/ *Helena/* Em convênio com o Instituto Nacional do Livro/ Ministério da Educação e Cultura, sob o patrocínio do Programa de Ação Cultural do Departamento de Assuntos Culturais/ Civilização Brasileira/ 1975 [Edições Críticas de/ Obras de Machado de Assis/ Volume 2].

Machado de Assis's spelling of proper names has been retained: Helena, Valle, Estacio, et cetera.

# TRANSLATOR'S INTRODUCTION

Of Machado de Assis's nine novels the last five are by common consent rated his best. The novel *Helena* is not of that number. It is, however, and always has been, one of his most popular among Brazilian readers of all classes. Since its publication, in 1876, more than twenty editions have appeared in the original Portuguese.

There is perhaps good reason for such popularity. In other novels, Machado de Assis advanced his narrative through a poetico-lyrical medium of allusion, theme, symbolism, and dramatic shifts in emotion. In *Helena,* on the contrary, we find a sturdy plot cannily and meticulously contrived of dramatic acts on the part of the novel's principals, with suspense compounding suspense. In some respects this novel resembles a detective story. Helena herself, beautiful, talented, devoted and loyal but also strangely devious, is the source of the mystery with its dark implications of brother-sister incest. The priest Melchior, named for one of the Three Wise Men, tries to solve the mystery with his superior insight and priestly methods but is more wildly off scent than the most scientifically stupid prefect of police that ever was; thundering divine law, he accuses the wrong suspects. And the story's denouement, like any good whodunit's, is precisely what no one expected.

Along with its suspenseful action, *Helena* has another attraction for its readers: it is romantic. In his foreword to the 1905 edition, Machado de Assis warns: "Do not blame me for anything romantic you may find in it." But who will blame him? As Anatole Broyard has recently written, "It is difficult not to have a soft spot for romanticism."[1] *Helena* is unabashedly romantic. It is replete with "human hearts," "love," "feelings," "sentiments," "souls," "agitation," "anguish," "honor," "longing," and "regret." Women are supposed to be modest, submissive, and seductive; men, virile and magnanimous. The scene is Rio de Janeiro, 1850, a time when those sorts of things were de rigueur; and the book published in 1876 when they were still eagerly accepted.

It is a rarefied atmosphere, and our hero and heroine are idealized, but warm-blooded for all that. Helena *is* modest, submissive, and seductive. At the same time, she is highly intelligent, artistically talented and capable, passionately proud, and passionate in her love and devotion. She can also be gentle and understanding; she is regularly vivacious and witty. Her past, however, is cloaked in romantic mystery, to which she herself adds with strange secret behavior and with enigmatic sighs and half-words.

In true romantic style this heroine and her hero, Estacio do Valle, are spiritually destined for each other by some higher power:

> At first it was a simple meeting of the eyes, but within a few seconds it was something more. It was the first revelation, tacit but conscious, of the feeling that bound them together. Neither of them had sought this coming together of souls but neither shrank from it. What they said with their eyes alone cannot be written on paper, cannot be repeated for human ears — a secret, mysterious confession made from one heart to the other, heard only in heaven because it was not said in the language of earth, nor did they speak for this earth. Their hands of themselves joined, as their glances had; no shame, no fear, no consideration held back that fusion of two beings born to form a single existence.

---

[1] *New York Times*, October 17, 1982, Y-13.

Although the plot rests on Helena, it is Estacio's story: our sympathy fearfully accompanies him as he tries to solve the mystery attaching to Helena and, without being aware of it, falls more and more deeply in love with her in the process. Helena holds the key to the mystery but because of her conflicting loyalties will not reveal it, and is forced, or forces herself, upon paths of deceit. No one knows her history. The author does not permit us to know the workings of her mind. We are allowed to see her actions and hear her conversation; we see her smile and weep, but we are never privy to her thoughts.

With Estacio it is quite otherwise: his every thought and feeling, his doubts and hopes, are all presented in detail. He is of an open, generous nature, a gentleman, considerate, warm, and tender. He is one of the most attractive male characters Machado de Assis ever created. The 1905 foreword mentions the novel's "echo of youth and ingenuous faith." Is the author referring to this hero with whom, perhaps, he himself identified and to the idyllic life on the Valle chácara, a country estate on the outskirts of Rio de Janeiro? Although Machado de Assis was of humble origin —his father the son of freed slaves, a painter-decorator by trade, his mother a Portuguese immigrant from the Azores —he passed his earliest years on just such an estate belonging to his wealthy godmother, where his parents then lived as dependents. In *Helena* the chácara is a romantic haven of peace and beauty. Machado de Assis's other fiction is almost devoid of mention of external nature. This novel dwells lovingly on the chácara's trees and flowers in the changing light.

But what of life beyond the chácara? Out there is Society. It is the villain, with its laws that contravene the law of the human heart. And what is this Society to whose dictates all must bow? It is idle matrons with literary taste the author despises; it is a lawyer versed in the art of eating but ignorant of the law's tenets to his dying day; a military man who never succeeded in rising above the rank of major; in its upper echelon reigns a female arbiter of distinction, for she was "weaned by a modiste, a square dance was her first communion" and "her mind never outgrew its baby clothes." This society is gossiping schoolboys, gossiping card players, ladies sagacious in parlor romances, a grasping physician "who knew of nothing more serious than money" and for whom "all inconveniences are pleasant when they terminate in a legacy."

And yes, this society is the church, here represented by a respected priest. "Neither the law nor the Church is satisfied with the simple truth," says Father Melchior. And he insists the status quo must be maintained even though, as it happens, it may be a false position. "Scandal" is a word frequently on his lips; scandal must be avoided at all costs even if it means marriages of convenience. This priest is initially presented as an enlightened "modern day apostle," gentle, wise, sociable, tolerant, sure in his faith, constant in hope, ardent in charity; but soon other attributes appear and he proves to be a masterpiece of inconsistency—as if Machado de Assis sought to incorporate in the person of this one man all the contradictory beliefs and practices that had crept into the Church in the course of ages.

Melchior can be benevolent and understanding but also withdrawn and monkish, resenting intrusions upon his private meditations. He says his is a god of compassion and charity but conjures up a vengeful god of retribution. Forgetful of forbearance, he issues "imperious" commands and if necessary would resort to force. Though a profound scholar of the Christian philosophers, he indulges in superstitious rites, invoking the dead and demanding an oath on a crucifix, and he wonders if there might not be a curse on the house of Valle. He advocates the "straight way," but his ways are devious. "Since he was a sincere, open nature," we are told, "it was hard for him to believe in hypocrisy," and yet he finds "dissimulation a duty when sincerity is dangerous." He is said to embody the maxim "Unto the pure all things are pure," but he is suspicious and prying, with "curiosity" replacing what should have been "friendly interest." And his action based on false suspicions precipitates a catastrophe. Though the simplicity of his life is stressed, his robes and appearance inspire religious awe. He not only regards himself as a special emissary from heaven — "twice ordained, by nature and by the Gospel" — he even arrogates to himself the power of the deity, giving divine approval to an arranged marriage with the words "I am the voice of truth and infinite love." Although he pretends to represent divine law, he is actually the voice of society and temporal accommodation. He had made his peace with Counselor Valle's irregular way of life; he would now cause the son to maintain the false situation inherited from the father.

Had it not been for this priest's officious interference, Estacio, with the support of his simple, trusting aunt might have defied society in favor of his heart's desire; but there still would be Helena's pride to overcome. How contend with a pride so distrustful of his respect for her that their mutual love could not do away with it? — pride of a beautifully complex heroine that has enthralled Brazilian readers for more than a century.

May *Helena*'s new readers take the same pleasure in the story as they, and overlook its rough spots . . . awkward narrative transitions, sudden fortuitous entrances of characters on scene, melodramatic denouement. This novel does not exhibit the mastery of the medium one finds in a *Dom Casmurro* or a *Counselor Ayres' Memorial,* but it is still Machado de Assis, with an emotionally charged atmosphere, vibrant personages, dramatic strokes, irony, wit, and a beginning of the "symbolism that was to become an integral part of his later novels, with its subtle, poetic, pervasive strength."[2]

[2]Helen Caldwell, *Machado de Assis* (Berkeley, Los Angeles, London: University of California Press, 1970), p. 60.

# Helena

# FOREWORD [3]

This new edition of *Helena* goes forth with various emendations of language and other things, which do not alter the book's general aspect. It is of the same date as when I composed and published it, and thus quite different from what time has wrought of me since; it corresponds to the chapter of my spiritual history for the year 1876.

Do not blame me for anything romantic you may find in it. Of my writings from those days, this one is especially dear to me. Even now that I have long since gone to other works, of a different style, I hear a faraway echo on rereading these pages, an echo of youth and ingenuous faith. It is clear that in no case would I take from them their ancient aspect; each work belongs to its own time.

M. de A.

[3]Foreword to the 1905 edition: Machado de Assis/ (Da Academia Brasileira)/ *Helena*/ Nova edição/ H. Garnier, Livreiro-Editor/ 71 Rua do Ouvidor/ Rio de Janeiro/ 6, Rue des Saints-Pères/ Paris/ 1905.

# HELENA

## Chapter I

Counselor Valle died at seven o'clock on the night of April
25, 1850. He died of a sudden stroke of apoplexy shortly
after his siesta of forty winks (as he used to call it) while he
was getting ready to go play the usual game of ombre at
the home of a supreme court judge, a friend of his. Dr.
Camargo, summoned in haste, did not arrive in time to
offer the assistance of science; Father Melchior was too late
to give him the consolations of religion. Death had been
instantaneous.

The funeral, however, which took place on the following
day, was one of the best attended ever seen by the residents
of Andarahy. About two hundred persons accompanied
the deceased to his final residence, among them a goodly
representation of society's upper classes. Although the
counselor may not have figured prominently in great
affairs of state, he did occupy a lofty position in society,
through connections he had formed, wealth, good breeding, and an old family name. His father had been a magis-
trate in colonial times and a person of some influence at
the court of the last viceroy. On his mother's side he was
descended from one of the most distinguished families in
São Paulo. He himself had held two government posts, in
which he conducted himself with adroitness and a dignified manner. This exemplary behavior brought him the
honorary title, Counselor to the Emperor, and the respect
of politicians. Notwithstanding the heated political climate

of those days, he was not affiliated with either of the two parties but preserved precious friendships in both, and these were on hand to lower him into his grave. Occasionally he did have political opinions of a sort, gathered on the frontiers of liberalism and conservatism at the exact point where the two dominions merge. But, if no partisan regret cast a last spade of earth on him, there was many a matron who saw interred with him the best page of her youth.

The counselor's family consisted of two persons, a son, Estacio, and a sister, Dona Ursula. The latter was some fifty years old, unmarried, had always lived with her brother and had run his house for him since the death of her sister-in-law. Estacio was twenty-seven, with a degree in mathematics. His father had tried to steer him into politics and then into a diplomatic career, but neither of those projects made any headway.

When Dr. Camargo, their family physician and old friend, returned from the funeral, he went to call on Estacio and found him, with Dona Ursula, in the late counselor's private study. Grief has its pleasant side: aunt and nephew sat nursing it with the presence of the dead man's personal belongings, there in his favorite daily haunt. The little room was lighted by two wretched candles. Several seconds passed in profound silence. The doctor was the first to speak.

"Did your father leave a will?"

"I don't know," Estacio answered.

Camargo bit the tip of his moustache two or three times, a habitual gesture when he was reflecting.

"You should try to find it," he went on. "Would you like me to help you?"

Estacio warmly grasped his hand. "My father's death," he said, "has in no way altered our relations. There will always be the same trust as in the past, the same friendship, tried and of long standing."

The secretary was locked. Estacio gave the doctor the key, and he unlocked it with no outward sign of emotion. Inwardly he was greatly perturbed. What *was* visible was the lively expression of curiosity in his eyes; but neither of the other two noticed it. As soon as he started to leaf through the papers his hand trembled with feverish haste. When he found the will his eyes lighted up for just a second, then resumed their usual look of serene calm.

"Is that it?" asked Estacio.

Camargo did not answer immediately. He looked at the document as if trying to divine its contents. His silence was so prolonged that it could not fail to make an impression on Estacio, but the young man said nothing, for he attributed it to a friend's natural emotion in such sad circumstances.

"Do you know what may be inside this?" Camargo finally said. "Possibly an omission, or some great excess . . ."

Neither Estacio nor Dona Ursula asked the doctor for an explanation of this remark. Their curiosity, however, was natural and he read it in their eyes but said nothing. Without a word, he handed the will to Estacio, got up and walked about the room, absorbed in his own thoughts, now mechanically straightening a book on its shelf, now sticking the tip of his moustache between his teeth, his eyes vacant, his mind far away from the little room and its occupants.

Estacio broke the silence: "What do you mean 'omission or excess'?"

Camargo stopped in front of him. "I must not say," he answered. "It would be improper before we know what final bequests your father made."

Dona Ursula was less discreet than her nephew. After a long pause she asked the doctor the reason for his remark.

"Your brother," he replied, "was a good soul. I had opportunity to know him intimately and to appreciate his fine qualities. I was his friend; I feel sure he was mine.

Nothing altered our long friendship nor the trust we both placed one in the other. I would not wish, therefore, that the last act of his life be an error."

"An error!" exclaimed Dona Ursula.

"Possibly an error!" sighed Camargo.

"But, doctor," insisted Dona Ursula, "why do you not set our minds at rest? Surely it is not a question of anything that would bring dishonor on my brother's name. You are probably alluding to some error in judgment... something... I have no idea what it might be... Why don't you speak plainly?"

The doctor recognized that Dona Ursula was right and that if he refused to say more it would have been better to have kept quiet in the first place. He tried to dispel the unpleasant sense of mystery he had aroused in their minds. But, from the hesitating manner in which he spoke, Estacio concluded that he *could* not go beyond what he had already said, and the young man interrupted him: "There is no need for any explanation. Tomorrow we shall know everything."

The doctor left at ten o'clock, promising to return early the next day. As Estacio retired to his room he muttered to himself, "What is this *error* of his? What could it be? And why did he have to trouble me with this enigma?"

The answer, if he had been able to hear it, was given at that very moment by Dr. Camargo himself, as he stepped into his carriage, which was waiting for him at the door. "I did right in preparing their minds," he mused; "the blow, if it is to fall, will be easier for them to bear."

The physician was alone; besides, it was night, as we know. No one could have seen the expression on his face; it was gathered in a meditative scowl as he exhumed the past and held an inquest over the future; but nothing of all that he saw and foresaw was communicated to other ears.

Dr. Camargo's relations with the counselor's family were close and of long standing, as Estacio had said. The physician and the counselor were the same age, fifty-four. They had met soon after leaving the university, and from that time the bond between them had never weakened.

Camargo, at first sight, was not very charming. His features were hard and cold, his eyes penetrating and knowing with a penetration that disconcerted and repelled whoever encountered their gaze. He spoke little, and that in a flat, harsh tone. His feelings were never revealed in his countenance. He had all the outward marks of a complete egoist, and yet, although the counselor's death could not wrench a tear from him, or a word of sorrow, it is certain that he truly felt it. Add to that, he loved above everything and everybody one beautiful creature, the beautiful Eugenia, as he called her, his only daughter and the apple of his eye; but he loved her with a silent, secret love. It would be difficult to say whether Camargo subscribed to any political opinions or nourished feelings of a religious nature. As for the former, if he had them he never showed it in any way; and during the struggles that had filled the preceding decade he had kept aloof and neutral. As for religious sentiments, to judge from his actions, no one possessed more genuine ones; he was punctual in the performance of the duties of a good Catholic. But punctual was all; at heart he was a nonbeliever.

When Camargo arrived home in Rio Comprido, he found his wife, Dona Thomazia, half asleep in a rocking chair, and Eugenia at the piano, playing over a passage of Bellini. Eugenia had talent and Camargo loved to hear her play; but, at such a time, he said, it was not seemly for her to give way to any kind of enjoyment. Eugenia submitted, though somewhat reluctantly. As she rose from her place at the piano, her father caught hold of her hands and looked at her in a way she had never seen before, intently, with eyes full of love.

"I didn't grieve," she remarked, "because you told me not to, papa. I was playing to take my mind off my sadness.

Dona Ursula . . . how is she? She was so overcome! Mama wanted to stay longer, but I confess I could not endure seeing the sorrow in that house."

"Sorrow is a necessity of life," asserted Dona Thomazia. She had opened her eyes at her husband's entrance. "The sufferings of others remind us of our own and serve as a corrective to happiness, an excess of which can engender pride."

Camargo tempered this philosophy, which seemed a little austere to him, with some ideas that were more comfortable and cheerful. "Let us grant each age its proper climate," he concluded, "and not anticipate the time of reflection and so render unhappy those who have not yet passed beyond a state of pure sentiment."

Eugenia did not understand what they were talking about. Her eyes turned back to the piano with a look of regret and longing. And, even as she stood, her left hand absently drew forth three or four notes from the beloved keys. Camargo looked at her again with that strange tenderness; his somber face glowed as if lighted by a radiance from within. His daughter felt herself enclosed in his arms and yielded to the embrace. But this expansiveness of his was so novel, so unprecedented that she was startled and asked in a tremulous voice, "Did something happen there, in Andarahy?"

"No! Not a thing! Nothing at all!" he replied, and he placed a kiss on her forehead.

It was the first kiss he had ever given her, at least the first she had any memory of. The caress gratified her filial pride, but the novelty of it made a still greater impression. She did not believe what her father had just said to her. She saw him go sit by Dona Thomazia and converse with her in an undertone. When Eugenia drew near they did not break off their conversation but went on talking in the same low tone — discussing purely domestic affairs, as it turned out. Even so, Eugenia's mind was not set at ease.

The next morning she wrote a note that immediately sped on its way to Andarahy. The reply arrived as she was trying on a new dress, but it had the courtesy to wait until she concluded that important operation. When it was finally read it dispelled her fears of the night before.

*Chapter II*

Later that day, the will was opened with all the legal formalities. The counselor named Estacio, Dr. Camargo, and Father Melchior executors. There was nothing remarkable about the provisions in general: there were religious and charitable bequests, remembrances to friends, marriage portions for his godchildren, masses for his soul and for the souls of his relatives.

There was one provision, however, of major importance. The counselor declared that he recognized a natural daughter named Helena, born to him by Dona Angela da Soledade. This young girl was being educated at a boarding school in Botafogo. She was named heir to her proper share of his wealth and was to go live with his family, whom he urgently begged to treat her with gentle care and affection, just as though she had been born in wedlock.

The reading of this provision naturally astonished the dead man's sister and his son. Dona Ursula had never heard of any such daughter. As for Estacio, he was less ill-informed than his aunt. He had once heard a daughter of his father's talked of, but so vaguely that he would not have expected this provision in the will.

In both aunt and nephew astonishment soon gave place to another and different feeling. Dona Ursula disapproved the counselor's act in toto. It seemed to her that, in spite of natural instincts and legal regulations, the recognition of

Helena was an act of encroachment and a very bad example. This new daughter was, in her view, an intruder without any right to her relatives' love. She agreed that she should be given her share of the inheritance and then shown the door. But to receive her into the bosom of the family and its chaste affections, to legitimize her in the eyes of society as she had been in the eyes of the law . . . Dona Ursula simply did not understand it, nor did she see how anyone could. The asperity of these sentiments became even greater when she happened to think of Helena's possible origin. Nothing was known of the mother except her name. But who was she? In what shady bypath of life had the counselor met her? Was Helena the daughter of a chance encounter or was she born of a single attachment — irregular but genuine and constant? Dona Ursula found no answers to these questions, but the mere fact that they cropped up in her mind was enough to disgust and exasperate her.

Dona Ursula had very strict ideas about moral behavior. The counselor's life, a colorful text of gallant adventures, was far from being a page out of the Catechism; but this final act of his might well be reparation for his offensive indiscretions. Dona Ursula, however, did not see it as an extenuating circumstance. For her the main thing was the admission of a stranger into the family.

Estacio's feeling was far different. He had noted the ill will with which his aunt received the news of Helena's recognition, and he had to admit to himself that a thing like this did create a strange situation for the family. Nevertheless, whatever she might be, once his father had so ordered it, whether led by a sense of justice or by a natural impulse, Estacio was ready to accept her, no matter what, without regret, without reservation. The question of the money weighed less than all else to his way of thinking; it had no weight at all. The occasion was too sad to admit considerations of an inferior order, and Estacio's high-mindedness would not have permitted him to do so in any event. As for the social stratum to which Helena's mother had belonged, he did not give it much thought, persuaded that they, his aunt and he, would be able to raise the daughter into the class she was now supposed to enter. In the midst of his reflections on the clause in the will, there recurred to him the conversation he had had with Dr. Camargo. Probably that was what the doctor was alluding to. Questioned about it, Camargo hesitated, but when Estacio insisted:

"Just what I foresaw has occurred—an error. There was no omission, only excess. The recognition of that daughter is an excess of tenderness, very fine, very handsome, but not at all practical. Strict justice..."

"Strict justice," Estacio quickly interposed, "is my father's wish."

"Your father was generous," said Camargo. "It remains to be seen whether he may have been so at the cost of another's rights."

"Mine? I do not assert them."

"If you did you would be unworthy of his memory. 'What is done, is done.' Now that she has been recognized the girl must find, in this house, family and family affection. I am persuaded that she will be able to respond with genuine devotion."

"You know her?" Estacio fixed his eyes on him with a look of impatient curiosity.

"I saw her three or four times," the doctor replied after a slight hesitation, "but she was then a very small child. Your father used to tell me about her. She was an extremely affectionate girl, he said, worthy of being loved and admired. A father's eyes perhaps!"

Estacio would have liked to learn something about Helena's mother, but he felt a reluctance to pursue the investigation further and attempted to steer the conversation into another quarter. Camargo meanwhile continued the subject:

"The counselor spoke to me a number of times about his plan to recognize Helena. I sought to dissuade him, but you know how stubborn he was, and in this case even more so from a natural instinct of paternal love. Our points of view differed widely. I do not consider myself an illiberal man; nevertheless, I believe sensibility ought not arrogate to itself the prerogatives of reason."

Camargo uttered these words in the flat, sententious tone that regularly poured out of him so easily and naturally. The longtime friendship that existed between him and the deceased was known to them all. Could it be possible that he had spoken as an unfriendly critic? Estacio reflected a while on the moral concept he had just heard from the doctor's lips. It was a brief reflection and in no way weakened the opinion he himself had formed and given voice to shortly before. His eyes, large and tranquil, like the generous spirit that animated them, rested benevolently on the speaker.

"I have no desire," said he, "to know whether or not there is excess in the provisions of my father's will. If there is, it is legitimate, justifiable at least. He knew what it was to be a father; his love, though divided, remained whole. I will receive this sister as if she had been brought up with me. My mother would certainly have done the same."

Camargo did not persevere. In addition to its being a useless exertion to try to change the young man's sentiments, what would he gain by discussing and theoretically condemning the counselor's arrangement? It would be better to carry out the provisions loyally, without delay, without questioning. He said as much to Estacio, who hugged him with heartfelt emotion. The doctor received the embrace without embarrassment but without enthusiasm.

For his part, Estacio was content. He derived his disposition more directly from his mother than from his father. The counselor—if we discount the one strong passion of his life, that is, his passion for women—we shall find had no other salient feature. His loyalty to his friends was more the result of habit than of any constancy in his affections. His life flowed smoothly along without crises, without ups and downs; he never found a need to test his own mentality. If he had he would have discovered that it was mediocre.

Estacio's mother was far different. She possessed in high degree ardent love, gentleness, strength of will, refined feelings with their touches of pride — pride that was merely the reflected rays of self-respect. Though chained to a man who, in spite of her love for him, frittered away his heart's treasure on passing, adventitious amours, she had the necessary will power to dominate her love and lock all resentment within her. In such circumstances, women who are no more than women weep, sulk, or become resigned; women who have something more than feminine softness fight or withdraw into the dignity of silence. This woman suffered, it is certain, but her nobility of spirit allowed her no other course but one of proud silence. At the same time, as affection was an essential element of her nature, she concentrated it all on that only son, in whom she saw the heir of her own robust qualities.

As a matter of fact, Estacio had inherited from her a large share of those qualities. Having no great talent, he owed to will power and his passion for learning the considerable figure he cut among his classmates. He applied himself to science with fervor and genuine devotion. He detested politics and scorned the noisy bustle of the outside world. Brought up with severity and modesty in the old-fashioned manner, he passed from adolescence to manhood without knowing corruptions of spirit or the pernicious influence of idleness; he lived within the family at an age when his companions were living in the streets and losing, among base things, the virginity of their first sensations. Hence at eighteen years of age he still had a certain boyish diffidence that he lost only some time later. Even then, he retained a certain gravity which was not unbecoming to his youthful years and very proper to one of his temperament. In politics it would probably have carried him halfway along the road to important public trusts; in society it caused people to have respect for him and thus elevated him in his own eyes. One should explain that this gravity of his was not the heavy, boring, vulgar thing that the moral philosophers tell us is almost always a symptom of an empty mind. It was genial, easy, equally remote from frivolity and from tediousness, a sedate composure of mind and body, tempered by an exuberance of feeling and by gracious manners: it was an upright, rigid trunk adorned with foliage and flowers. Joined to his other spiritual qualities, Estacio possessed a sensibility that was neither effeminate nor sickly but sober and strong; strict with himself, he could be mild and gentle with others.

Such was the counselor's son. If anything else is to be added, it is that he never yielded nor forgot any of the rights and obligations conferred upon him by his age and the class into which he had been born. Elegant and polished, he obeyed the law of personal decorum even in its lesser forms. No one entered a drawing room more correctly; no one left it more opportunely. He was not versed in the art of small talk, but he knew the secret of weaving a compliment.

In the situation created by the counselor's will, Estacio accepted his sister's cause and viewed her, without knowing her, with eyes far different from Camargo's and Dona Ursula's. Dona Ursula recounted to her nephew all the impressions left upon her by her brother's act. Estacio attempted to do away with them: he repeated what he had said to the doctor; he pointed out that after all it was a matter of fulfilling a last wish of the dead.

"I am well aware that there is now no other remedy but to accept this child and obey my brother's solemn instructions," said Dona Ursula when Estacio finished speaking. "But only that! Share my affections with her? I am not sure that I could, or that I ought to."

"Still, she is of our blood."

Dona Ursula shrugged her shoulders as if refusing to admit any such consanguinity. Estacio went on trying to bring her into a more benevolent frame of mind. He invoked not only *the last wish* but also his father's just and upright nature, which would never have permitted him to make any disposition that was inconsistent with family honor.

"Besides, the girl is not to blame for her origin, and in view of the fact that my father legitimized her she should not be made to feel like a foundling. What would we gain by that? It would only disturb the tranquility of our intimate family life. Let us go on sharing our affection with one another; and let us see in Helena a share of my father's soul left to us that the common patrimony might in no way be diminished."

The counselor's sister made no reply. Estacio understood that he had not overcome his aunt's feelings, nor was it possible to do so by means of words. He entrusted that task to time. Dona Ursula remained gloomy and withdrawn. When Camargo called soon after, she confided to him her whole view of the matter, of which the doctor privately approved.

"Did you know her mother?" she asked.

"Yes."

"What kind of woman was she?"

"Fascinating."

"That's not what I asked. I mean, was she a woman of lower class, or . . . ?"

"I don't know. At the time I saw her she was of no particular class and could have belonged to any class. Besides, I didn't know her very well."

"Doctor," said Dona Ursula after a few moments, "what do you advise me to do?"

"To love her, if she deserves it, and if you can."

"Oh! I confess that it will be hard for me, very hard! And will she deserve it? Something within me tells me that this child has come to complicate our life; what's more I cannot forget that my nephew, the heir..."

"Your nephew accepts the whole thing philosophically and even with satisfaction. I do not understand the satisfaction, but I agree that there is nothing else to be done but carry out the counselor's wishes to the letter. There is no arguing with sentiments: one loves or one hates, as the heart wills. My advice to you is, treat her with kindness, and, if you should feel within you some bit of affection, do not smother it, yield to it. There is no turning back now. Unfortunately!"

Helena was in her last days of school. Some weeks later the family arranged for her to come home to them. Dona Ursula at first refused to go after her; her nephew convinced her that she should, and the good lady accepted the obligation after some hesitation. Quarters in the house were readied for the young lady, and a certain Monday afternoon was set for her to be brought to Andarahy. Dona Ursula got into the carriage right after dinner. Estacio dined that day with Dr. Camargo in Rio Comprido. He returned late. On entering the grounds, he turned his eyes toward the windows of the bedroom that was to be Helena's; they were open; there was someone inside. For the first time, Estacio felt the strangeness of the situation created by that half sister's presence, and he asked himself if his aunt was not the one who was in the right. He immediately rejected the thought; remembrance of his father restored his earlier benevolence. At the same time, the idea of having a sister made his heart leap up with its promise of new, unknown fortunes. Between his mother and all other women he had known, he felt the want of that intermediary being, whom he already loved though he had never met her; she would be the natural confidante of his disappointments and hopes. Estacio remained looking at the windows for a long time, but Helena's form did not appear there. He did not see even a fleeting shadow of the new lodger.

## *Chapter III*

The next morning Estacio rose late and went straight to the dining room where he found Dona Ursula sitting placidly in her comfortable easy chair by the window, reading a tome of *St. Clair of the Isles*[4] and for the hundredth time melted to pity by the sorrows of the outlaws on the Isle of Barra: excellent folk and most moral book, even though tedious and heavy. The matrons of that age used it to kill many long winter hours, fill many a quiet evening, and unbosom the heart of its surplus of tears.

"Did she come?" asked Estacio.

"Yes," replied the good lady, closing her book. "Breakfast is getting cold," she added, addressing the *mucama*[5] who stood by the table. "Have they called . . . Nhanhan Helena?"

"Nhanhan Helena said she was coming."

"That was ten minutes ago," observed Dona Ursula to her nephew.

"She probably won't be long," he replied. "What's she like?"

Dona Ursula was not really in a position to answer her nephew's question. She had seen almost nothing of Helena's face, and as soon as they reached home the girl withdrew to the quarters they had given her, saying she needed to rest. All that Dona Ursula could say for certain was that her niece was a full grown young lady.

A quick step was heard descending the stairs, and then Helena appeared in the doorway to the dining room. Estacio was leaning against the window opposite, which gave on the veranda at the rear of the house and the grounds of

[4]*St. Clair of the Isles, or, The Outlaws of Barra, a Scottish tradition,* by Elizabeth Helme (London: T. N. Longman and O. Rees, 1803). Dona Ursula probably read it in translation.

[5]*mucama,* a Brazilian term for a favorite young female slave employed about the house.

the chácara[6] stretching beyond it. He glanced at his aunt as if waiting for her to introduce them to each other. Helena stood still on seeing him.

"Child," said Dona Ursula in the sweetest tone she could summon from her vocal chords, "this is my nephew Estacio, your brother."

"Ah!" said Helena, smiling and walking toward him.

He had taken a few steps in *her* direction.

"I hope to be worthy of your affection," she said after a short pause. "Please forgive me for being late. I am afraid I have kept you waiting . . ."

"We were just sitting down this very moment," interposed Dona Ursula as if protesting against the idea that Helena had made them wait.

Estacio hastened to soften his aunt's rudeness. "We heard your step on the stairs," he explained. "Come, let us sit down, breakfast will be getting cold."

Dona Ursula had already taken her place at the head of the table. Helena sat at her right in the chair indicated to her by Estacio. He seated himself across from her. Breakfast proceeded in dreary silence; occasional monosyllables, mute signs of acceptance or refusal; that was the total disbursement of conversation by the three relatives. The situation was not a comfortable one nor at all what is usual. Although Helena strove to maintain her self-composure, she did not wholly succeed in overcoming a shyness that was quite natural under the circumstances. But in her very confusion there appeared sure tokens of good breeding.

Estacio examined his sister's person point by point. She was a young woman of sixteen or seventeen, slender without being thin, a little above medium height, elegant figure. Her cheeks, a dark peach color, had the same imperceptible down as that fruit; on this occasion they had

---

[6]*chácara*, a country estate on the edge of the city.

traces of a deep rose, almost red at first, natural effect of her emotion. The pure, severe lines of her face seemed a work of religious art. If her brown hair, instead of being gathered in two thick braids, had fallen loose over her shoulders, and if her brown eyes had raised their pupils to heaven, you would have said she was one of those adolescent angels that used to bring the Lord's messages to Israel. Art could not have exacted greater correctness and harmony of features; and society might well be content with her polished manners and grave air. One thing alone seemed less pleasing to her brother: the eyes, or rather their glance with its expression of furtive curiosity and suspicious reserve; it was the only blemish that he found in her but it was not a small one.

Breakfast over, a few phrases exchanged, brief and disconnected, Helena withdrew to her room; and there, for three days, she passed almost every hour, reading the half-dozen books she had brought with her, writing letters, gazing listlessly into the air or leaning on the window sill. One time she came down to dinner with red eyes and sorrowful look, a wan, fleeting smile on her lips. A little girl suddenly transplanted to boarding school would not have shed her first homesick longings in greater wretchedness. But time's wing bears away everything, and at the end of three days Helena's countenance already wore a less somber aspect. Her glance had lost the expression her brother first found in it and had become, what it was by nature, gentle and reposeful. Her words came forth more easily, in sequence and profusion; friendly confidence took the place of shyness.

On the fourth day, after breakfast, Estacio started a general conversation that did not pass beyond a simple duo, because Dona Ursula was busy counting the threads in the tablecloth or playing with the tips of her neckerchief.

In speaking of the house, Estacio said to his sister, "This house is as much yours as ours, just as though you and I had been born under the same roof. My aunt will tell you what feelings we nourish in regard to you."

Helena thanked him with a look that was earnest and intense. And, remarking that the house and the chácara seemed to her handsome and well ordered, she asked Dona Ursula to show them to her in more detail.

Her aunt frowned and answered coldly, "Not now, child; it is my time to rest and read."

"Then I will read to you," the girl rejoined sweetly. "It's not good for you to tire your eyes, and besides it is right for me to get in the habit of waiting on you. Don't you agree?" she added, turning to Estacio.

"She is our aunt," he answered.

"Oh! she is not yet mine!" interrupted Helena. "She will be when she gets to know me. For the time being, we are strangers to each other; but neither of us has a bad nature." These words were said in a tone of graceful sub-mission. The voice with which she uttered them was clear, gentle, and melodious; better still, it had a mysterious charm that even Dona Ursula could not resist.

"Then let our life together make our hearts speak," the counselor's sister replied in a mild tone. "I do not accept your offer to read to me, because I have difficulty under-standing what others read; my eyes are more intelligent than my ears. But if you wish to see the house and the chá-cara, your brother will serve as your guide."

Estacio declared himself ready to accompany his sister. Helena, however, refused his offer. Though her brother, he was new to her, and also, it seemed, it would be the first time for her to be alone with a man who was not her father. Dona Ursula, perhaps because she wanted to be alone for a while, coldly told her to go with him. Helena accompanied her brother. They went over part of the house, the young girl listening to Estacio's explanations and eagerly inquir-ing into everything with the curiosity of a housewife. When they came to the door of the counselor's study, Estacio stopped.

"We are about to enter a room that is full of sadness for me," he said.

"What is it?"

"My father's study."

"Oh! let me see!"

They went in, the two of them. Everything was exactly the same as on the day the counselor died. Estacio told her something of his father's habits and home life. He showed her the chair where he used to sit reading in the afternoon and of a morning; the family portraits, the secretary, and book cases; he spoke of all that might interest her. On the table near the window the last book the counselor had read still lay open: it was the *Maxims* of the Marquis de Maricá. Helena picked it up and kissed the open page. Tears rose to her eyes, tears hot with the ardor of a passionate, sensitive nature, and a bead slipped from its lash and fell on the paper. "Poor dear," she murmured. Then she sat on the chair in which the counselor used to sleep for a few minutes after dinner, and she gazed out the window.

The day was becoming warm. The grove on the opposite hills was covered with Lenten flowers, sadly beautiful in their purple petals; the scene went with the mood of both brother and sister. Estacio let himself go at the beck of childhood memories. Mingling with them his mother's form appeared to him; he saw her again as she was when she slipped away in his arms on a cruel night in October, when he was eighteen. She died almost young, still beautiful at least, with the beauty that has no autumn, but only a second springtime.

Helena got up. "Were you fond of him?" she asked.

"Who wouldn't be?"

"You are right. He was a great, noble soul. I adored him. He recognized me, gave me a family and future, elevated me in the eyes of the world and in my own eyes. The rest depends on me, on my good sense, or perhaps on chance." This last word was breathed as a sigh from the heart. After a few moments of silence Helena linked her arm in her brother's and they went down to the chácara.

Whether it was the influence of the place or simply mobility of temperament, Helena now became a different person from the one she had been in her father's study; laughing, full of charm and mischief, she also lost the quiet gravity and self-composure with which she had appeared in the dining room. She became quick and lively, like the swallows that before and even now were darting among the trees and over the grassy meadows. The change somewhat amazed her brother, but he explained it to himself to his own satisfaction; at least it did not make a bad impression upon him. Helena now seemed to him, even more than before, the proper complement to their family. What it had lacked hitherto was this very birdsong of chatter, this charm and playfulness, an element to temper the austerity of the house and give it the necessary features of a home. Helena was that complementary element.

Their walk lasted about half an hour. At the end of that time Dona Ursula saw them return son and daughter of the same family, and friends, as if they had grown up together. Her gray brows gathered in a frown and her lower lip received a sharp bite of annoyance.

"Aunty . . . ," said Estacio cheerily, "my sister now knows the whole house and its outbuildings; it only remains for us to show her our hearts."

Dona Ursula smiled, a thin, tight smile that extinguished in the girl's eyes the happiness that had made them so beautiful. But the bad impression was brief; she walked up to her aunt, took her hands, and asked in a voice that was all gentleness, "Won't you show me yours?"

"It's not worth the trouble!" retorted Dona Ursula with affected good humor. "An old woman's heart is a tumbledown house."

"But old houses can be fixed up," rejoined Helena with a smile.

Dona Ursula also smiled, this time with a kinder expression, and she looked at Helena attentively; it was the first time she had done so. Her glance, at first indifferent, soon showed the impression caused by the girl's beauty. Dona Ursula withdrew here eyes; perhaps she feared that the influx of Helena's graces would twist her heart, and she wanted to remain independent and unreconciled.

## Chapter IV

The first weeks slipped by without any remarkable occurrence, and yet it was an interesting time. It was, so to speak, a time of waiting, of hesitating, of reciprocal observation and sounding of character while each sought to become familiar with the terrain and take up a position. Even Estacio, notwithstanding his first impression, had retreated into a careful reserve out of which Helena's ways had to coax him little by little. She had the proper talents to take captive the family's confidence and affection. She was docile, affable, intelligent. Neither these gifts, however, nor her beauty were her most effective weapons. What made her exceptional and gave her a good chance of victory was her art of accommodating herself to the circumstances of the moment and to every type of mind, a precious art, which makes men successful and women admired. She would talk of books or pins or fancy balls or household goods, with the same interest and style, frivolous with the frivolous, grave and serious with those who were grave and serious, attentive and well-spoken without either loftiness or vulgarity. She had a little girl's lightheartedness and the self-possession of a woman, a perfect harmony of homely virtues and elegant manners.

Besides her natural qualities, Helena possessed certain social gifts that made her well received everywhere, and partly changed the family's way of life. I am not speaking of her magnificent contralto voice nor the correctness with which she had learned to use it, because the counselor's memory being still fresh, there had been no opportunity for it to be heard. She was an excellent pianist, was good at drawing and sketching, spoke French fluently, and a little English and Italian, was skilled in sewing and embroidery and all types of women's work. She conversed with witty grace, and read to perfection. Thanks to these resources and to great patience, art, and a submissiveness that was not humble but self-respecting, she had succeeded in smoothing the rough ones, attracting the indifferent, and taming the hostile.

The gains made over Dona Ursula's mind were few, but resistance from that quarter was not so rigorous as it had been in the first days. Estacio surrendered completely. He was an easy conquest; his heart had already reached out to her far more than any of the others. He did not yield, however, without some hesitancy and doubt. His sister's flexibility of spirit at first seemed to him more calculated than spontaneous. But it was an impression that passed. The slaves, too, held back. Helena did not immediately win their sympathy and good will; they gauged their feelings by those of Dona Ursula, and eyed with disfavor and jealousy this new kinswoman that had been brought into *their* family by an act of charity. But time won them over also. Of them all, only one was seen to look upon her with friendly eyes right from the start; it was a boy of sixteen named Vicente, born on the estate, and a special pet of the counselor's. Perhaps it was this last circumstance that attached him to her, his master's daughter. Without interest, for hope of freedom even if possible was uncertain and remote, Vicente's love was all the more strong and sincere. Lacking the usual joys of affection—familiarity and contact—condemned to live by contemplation and report and not even kiss the hand that blessed him, circumscribed and placed at a distance by custom, respect, and instinct, Vicente was nevertheless Helena's faithful servitor and her lawyer for the defense at the court sessions in the slaves' quarters.

The intimate friends of the family received Helena with the same hesitancy as Dona Ursula. Helena felt their cold, parsimonious courtesy. Far from feeling humiliated or reproaching society's sentiments, she tried to understand and turn them to her advantage, a task at which she excelled; overcoming the obstacles within the family, the rest would come of itself.

One person among the familiars of the house did not join in the cold, reserved behavior of the others, to wit, the cultivated priest, Father Melchior, the family chaplain. A few years before, the counselor had built him a little chapel on the estate, where many people of the neighborhood heard Mass on Sunday. He was sixty years old, a man of medium height, thin, bald with a few white hairs remaining, and with eyes no less wise than gentle. Of a quiet, grave bearing, he was austere but not formalistic, sociable without worldly sophistication, tolerant but not weak; he was a truly virile modern-day apostle, a man of his Church and of his God, sure in his faith, constant in hope, ardent in charity. He had become acquainted with the counselor's family shortly after the latter's marriage. He discovered the sadness that secretly tormented the last years of Estacio's mother; he respected her sorrow but made a direct attack on its cause. The counselor was a man ordinarily open to reason, save in matters of love. He listened to the priest, and promised what he exacted, but it was a promise written on sand; the first wind that stirred his heart obliterated the writing. And yet the counselor listened to him with sincerity on all other occasions, and Melchior's vote had great weight with him. The priest dwelt in the neighborhood of the family and it was his whole world. Except when ecclesiastical duties called him elsewhere, he did not stir out of Andarahy, a place of repose after an active life of toil.

Of the others who frequented the counselor's house and resided in the same suburb, Andarahy, we must also mention Dr. Mattos, his wife, and Colonel Macedo with his two children. Dr. Mattos was an old lawyer, who, in compensation for the science of jurisprudence, of which he had little or no knowledge, possessed very useful notions of meteorology and botany, the art of eating, ombre, backgammon, and politics. It was impossible for anyone to complain either of the heat or of the cold without hearing from him the cause and nature of one and the other, and of the division of the seasons, the different climates and their influence, the rains, the winds, snow, the silting of rivers and their floods, tides and the *pororoca*. He spoke with equal copiousness on the therapeutic qualities of an herb, the scientific name of a flower, the cell structure of a certain vegetable and its peculiarities. Averse to political passions, if he opened his mouth on that subject, it was to criticize in equal proportion both liberals and conservatives, all of whom he considered inferior to his country. Cards and food found him less skeptical; and nothing enlivened his physiognomy like a good game of backgammon after a good dinner. These talents made Dr. Mattos an interesting guest on evenings that were far from interesting. Granted that he really knew something of the subjects so prized by him, he had not acquired the wealth he possessed by giving instruction in botany or meteorology but by applying the tenets of the law, of which he was ignorant to his dying day.

Dr. Mattos' wife had been one of the beauties of the first empire. She was a faded rose but still preserved the aroma of youth. At one time, it was said, the counselor threw himself at her feet, aflame with love, without being repulsed by her; but only the first part of the rumor was true. Neither Dona Leonor's moral principles nor her temperament would have permitted her to do otherwise than repulse the counselor—without hurting his feelings, however. The art with which she did this deluded the malevolent; hence the whispered rumor, now dead and long forgotten. The reputation of amorous men is like compound interest: when a certain capital has been attained it multiplies by itself and grows bigger and bigger. The counselor enjoyed this advantage to such an extent that if all the transgressions they attributed to him on earth were to be placed to his account in the next world, he would receive twice the punishment he deserved.

Colonel Macedo had the distinguishing characteristic of not being a colonel. He was a major. Some of his friends, moved by a spirit of rectification, had conferred upon him the title of colonel, which he at first disclaimed but was finally compelled to accept, being unable to waste his entire life protesting against it. Macedo had seen and lived much, and, in addition to his hoard of experiences, had an imagination that was lively, fertile, and agreeable. He was a good companion, jolly and communicative, but capable of serious thought if it was necessary. He had two children, a young fellow of twenty who was at the university in São Paulo, and a daughter of twenty-three, more accomplished than beautiful.

By early August, it was plain, Helena's position was well established. Dona Ursula had not given in completely, but their life together was producing its fruit. Camargo alone remained unreconciled. One felt in his ceremonious politeness a profound aversion ready to change into hostility if need be. The rest of them were not only tamed but had even been placed under a spell; they had long since made peace with the counselor's daughter. She had become the event of the district: her sayings and attitudes were the topic of the neighborhood's conversation, and the delight of the family's regular visitors. From a natural curiosity, all searched their reminiscences for the young lady's biological link; but in these retrospective inventories no one could find material with which to construct the truth or even a sliver of it. Her origin continued mysterious; a great advantage, because the unknown fostered the myth, and each person could attribute Helena's birth to a highborn or a romantic love—both hypotheses admissible and each agreeable in its way.

## *Chapter V*

It was about this time that Estacio resolved to take a certain decisive step. Though engaged to Camargo's daughter since before the counselor's death, he kept hesitating to ask her father's consent, constantly putting it off to a more convenient and propitious moment. His situation was not an easy one, because his love for Eugenia fluctuated back and forth between lukewarm and fervent. The reason for this, as one may imagine, was partly in his own heart, but the main cause lay with her. He settled upon a certain day at the beginning of August to ask Eugenia for authorization to make the formal request of her father. With this intention, he left for Camargo's house.

As soon as Eugenia spied him from a distance, she went down to the garden gate. Her charming straw hat with wide brim to protect her face from the sun's rays—it was three o'clock in the afternoon—made her look all the more lovely. Eugenia was one of the brightest stars among those lesser stars in the Rio sky. Even today if you should catch a glimpse of her profile in a box at the theater, or see her enter a ballroom, you would understand, after a quarter of a century, why the friends of her youth praised, without compare, the graces then appearing in their dawn of freshness and purity. She was of small stature, had dark brown hair and big blue eyes, two bits of heaven's blue inserted into a pink and white visage. Her figure, only slightly remodeled, was naturally elegant; but, if its owner knew how to dress herself in a luxurious manner, and even with art, she did not possess the gift of attaining the maximum effect by the most simple means.

Estacio regarded her with adoring eyes, not venturing to say a word; the word that was about to burst from his lips was the very request that had brought him there. But Eugenia prevented him from uttering it by displaying the ring her godmother, a plantation mistress of Cantagallo, had sent her the day before. It was a magnificent opal, so magnificent that Eugenia divided her eyes between her lover and it. This simultaneous equivalency cooled the young man's ardor. Together they went into the house, where Dona Thomazia was expecting them. Eugenia's mother knew how to combine propriety with her heart's desires; *she* would not have been a hindrance to the pair of lovebirds. Unluckily the presence of a couple of visitors reduced to naught the calculations of all three. Estacio watched for a chance to ask Eugenia for the desired authorization; up to dinner time no such opportunity presented itself.

After dinner they all went down to the garden. Dona Thomazia entertained one of the guests; Camargo took the other to see his collection of flowers. Estacio and Eugenia quietly drew away from the two groups on the pretext of some flower or other that had bloomed that morning. The flower did exist; Eugenia plucked it and gave it to Estacio.

"Now don't lose it; you must give it to Helena from me. Tell her I miss her very much."

Estacio placed the flower in his buttonhole.

"It will fall out!" said Eugenia. "Want me to stick a pin in it?"

Estacio did not have time to answer because Camargo's daughter, taking a pin from her belt, began to secure the stem of the flower, wasting much more time than the operation called for. She did not suffer from myopia, and yet she brought her head so close to the young man's chest that he had an urge to kiss her hair, and it would have been the first time that his lips touched her.

"There!" said she. "Tell Helena that it is the prettiest flower in our garden. Do you know I am very fond of your sister?"

"I can well believe it."

"I think she is my friend; she has to be, surely. Oh! I need a true friend so much!"

"Yes?"

"So much! I have so many that are good for nothing and only cause me disappointments, like Cecilia . . . If you only knew what she did to me!"

"What did she do?"

Eugenia spun out a frivolous tale which I will omit in its particulars as having nothing to do with our business. Enough to know that the cause of the tiff had been a remark of Cecilia's concerning the choice of a hat.

Estacio did not listen to this story as attentively as the young lady would have liked; he confined himself to listening to her voice, which was really heavenly. Some of the story, however, did sink in, and when she had made an end of her complaints, he observed: "It seems to me that it was scarcely worth while to quarrel over such a little thing . . ."

"Little thing!" exclaimed Eguenia. "Does it seem to you a little thing for her to call me capricious and tasteless?"

"It was wrong of her, if she said that; but in any case . . ." Estacio paused and went on walking. Eugenia waited for him to finish what he was saying but his silence continued, unnaturally prolonged.

"In any case?" repeated Eugenia, raising limpid, inquiring eyes to his.

"Eugenia," said Estacio, "do you want to know the real reason for your bad luck with your friendships? It's because you allow yourself to be influenced by appearances rather than by real worth. It is because you place less value on the heart's solid qualities than on the frivolous superficialities of life. Your friendships are ones that last the whirl of a waltz or at most the fashion of a hat; they can satisfy the whim of a day but cannot answer the heart's demands."

"Good God!" exclaimed Eugenia, arresting her step, "a sermon for such a little thing! Add some Latin and it would be the same as listening to Father Melchior."

Estacio made no reply. He merely shrugged his shoulders, and both continued to walk on in silence, withdrawn and discontented with one another. The difference was that Eugenia's displeasure displayed itself in irritable gestures of impatience and resentment.

"If I offended you, please forgive me," she said in a lightly ironic tone.

"Oh!" he exclaimed, and he took her hand in his, as if only waiting for a pretext to resume the conversation that had been broken off.

"I probably did offend you," she went on. "I can only say things as they come into my head, and, it seems, they are not the wisest . . ."

"I don't say that is always so," rejoined Estacio, and he was smiling. "Just now, at least, it was a little hasty of you to scoff at what I was trying to tell you, which was honest and well intentioned. Frankly, is a friendship won between two quadrilles and lost over the fashion of a hat something to regret? It is not good to squander your affection, Eugenia; later you will come to understand that the heart's gold must never be reduced to small change or frittered away on gewgaws."

Eugenia heard him in silence; she did not understand much of what he said. She knew the meanings of the words but failed to see their connection or sense. What irritated her most was his pedagogical air. Capricious and headstrong, she did not allow anyone to speak to her except in a submissive and deferential manner, or to criticize actions of hers which *she* considered correct and natural. Estacio's insistence was the starting point of one of those petty quarrels not unusual between lovers and common between those two. Eugenia did not pout in silence. Her rebellious, unbridled spirit did not remain dormant in such moments of displeasure; on the contrary, she became more and more irritated, and her irritation appeared in fits of spite and bad temper. Estacio watched the storm rumble, gather, and break. The young lady uttered a few wild statements, stamped her darling little foot, which by chance crushed a miserable plant that knew nothing of the moral disagreements between those two creatures with legs. At first she checked her step and started to walk away, then she turned and went up to Estacio, her eyelids quivering with anger and a sarcastic remark on her lips, comforting herself by twisting the edge of her sleeve and biting the tip of her finger. Estacio, though accustomed to such explosions, knew of no appropriate remedy. Silence and soothing words were both inflammable materials in such circumstances. Silence, however, was the lesser of the two dangers. He limited himself to listening and saying nothing and looking at her out of the corner of his eye, for her face was still more beautiful when rage heightened its color. A third person was the only hope of peace. Estacio ran his eye over the garden in search of such a deus ex machina. The god appeared in the form of one Carlos Barreto, a medical student who was simultaneously cultivating pathology and comedy, but gave promise of being a better Aesculapius than Aristophanes. As soon as he caught sight of the pair he directed his steps toward them.

"Someone's coming, Eugenia," said Estacio. "Let's not make a scene and . . . forgive me."

Eugenia shrugged her shoulders and turned to see the newcomer, who in a few moments held out his hand to them.

The sky did not clear at once, but the wind fell; it was to be hoped the sun would finally lay aside his mantle of clouds. Carlos Barreto brought Eugenia the agreeable news that he had just given her father an invitation to a ball one of his relatives was to give on the following Saturday. The prospect of the ball was a favorable breeze that scattered the rest of the clouds; Eugenia smiled. *J'ai ri; me voilà désarmée,* as in Piron's comedy. Twenty minutes later Eugenia bore no vestige of the scene in the garden. But the marriage proposal had been postponed.

The result was bittersweet to Estacio. Though glad to see her anger dissipated, he was pained that it had not been because of her love but for a comparatively frivolous reason. His resolve to consult her about the formal request for her hand in marriage melted within him, as on previous occasions. He left in the evening, before tea, cross and irritated. This state did not last long; ten minutes after leaving Camargo's house he felt something like a sting of remorse. Estacio's love had the singular quality of increasing and gathering strength in absence and of diminishing as soon as he came into the lady's presence. From a distance he saw her through the luminous mist of his imagination; close by it was difficult for Eugenia to maintain possession of the graces he had lent her. Hence arose probable disagreement and certain remorse. Now that he had left her, he became angry with himself; he saw himself as petty and cruel. He ended by worshipping all Eugenia's charming triviality; he made allowances for her age, her upbringing, habits, and ignorance of life.

In this state of mind he arrived home...

## Chapter VI

...where he found a remedy for his bad humor in a letter from Luiz Mendonça, who had gone to Europe two years before, and was now returned. He wrote from Pernam-

buco, announcing that he would be in Rio de Janeiro within a few weeks. Mendonça had been Estacio's favorite
among his classmates. There was a wide difference in their
temperaments. Mendonça was more happy-go-lucky and
vivacious. When he was about to leave for Europe he
decided that his former schoolmate should go with him;
the counselor was of the same opinion. Estacio refused for
fear that, their natures being so different, travel together
would have obligated one of them to sacrifice his habits
and preferences.

The news of Mendonça's return filled him with joy.
Dona Ursula was in the sewing room, rereading some of
her *Saint Clair*. On the other side of the table, Helena was
putting the finishing touches to a piece of crochet.

"Aunty," said Estacio, "I have some news for you, most
agreeable news for me."

"What is it?"

"Mendonça has arrived in Pernambuco and will be here
in a few days."

"Mendonça?"

"Luiz Mendonça."

"The one who went to Europe, I remember. How long
ago was it?"

"Two years."

"Two years! It seems like yesterday."

"I won't read you his letter; it's too long. He says I must
go to Europe at once. Would you two ladies like to go?"

"I?" queried Dona Ursula, marking her place in the
book with the silver-rimmed spectacles that had been
perched on her nose up to then. "Old folks don't go chas-
ing off on holidays—just from here to the grave."

"Grave!" exclaimed Helena. "You are still hale and
hearty! Who knows if you won't be the one to bury me
first!"

"Oh, child!" cried Dona Ursula reproachfully.

Helena smiled happily, and gratefully; it was the first

word of genuine sympathy she had heard from Dona Ursula, as the latter well knew and perhaps was mortified by this spontaneous cry from the heart. But it was too late. She could not recall the words, she could not even explain them away.

"What will your friend be like now?" she asked her nephew. "He was a good lad before he went, a little crazy, that's all."

"He's sure to be the same," answered Estacio, "or better. Better, certainly, because two years will make a man more mature."

Estacio delivered a panegyric on his friend, intercalated with observations by his aunt and listened to in silence by his sister, until they were summoned to tea. Ursula laid aside her romance in earnest and Helena put away her crochet work in the sewing basket.

"You don't suppose I wasted the whole afternoon and evening on crochet, do you?" she asked her brother as they walked toward the dining room.

"No?"

"No, sir! I perpetrated a theft."

"Theft?"

"I took a book from your bookshelf."

"What book?"

"A novel."

"*Paul et Virginie*?"

"*Manon Lescaut*."

"Oh!" exclaimed Estacio. "That book..."

"Odd sort of book, isn't it? When I saw what it was like I closed it and put it back."

"It's not a book for young unmarried ladies..."

"Nor, I think, even for married ladies," Helena rejoined with a laugh as she took her place at table. "Anyway, I read only a few pages. Then I opened a geometry book... and, I confess, a desire came over me..."

"I can just imagine," interposed Dona Ursula.

"A desire to learn to ride horseback," concluded Helena.

Estacio looked at his sister in surprise. This mixture of geometry and equitation did not seem sufficiently clear and logical to him. Helena broke into a happy giggle, like a little girl applauding her own mischief.

"I will explain," said she. "I opened the book, which was all filled with lines and sketches I did not understand. Then I heard a clatter of horses' hooves and went to the window. There were three riders, two men and a lady. Oh! With what elegance the lady rode! Picture a young woman of twenty-five, tall, slender, a fairylike figure in a close-fitting riding habit with a long train falling to one side. The horse was spirited but her hand and her riding crop curbed its mettlesomeness. I admit, I felt a twinge of regret at not knowing how to ride . . ."

"Would you like me to teach you?"

"Aunty is willing?"

Dona Ursula shrugged her shoulders with the most indifferent air she could find in her whole repertoire. Helena waited for nothing further.

"You choose the day."

"Tomorrow?"

"Tomorrow."

Estacio was in the habit of going for a ride every morning. The next day's would be dispensed with; he would commence Helena's lessons. Before the lesson, however, very early that morning, he wrote Camargo's daughter a letter redolent of tenderness and affection. He begged forgiveness for what had passed the day before; he swore eternal love; all the things he had told her more than once, in the same style if not in the same words. The letter dispelled the last shadow of his remorse. Long before it arrived at its destination he had become completely reconciled to himself. The messenger left for Rio Comprido, and Estacio went down to the courtyard at the back of the house and adjoining the stable. Along that side of the house there ran an old-style veranda where the family sometimes took their coffee and conversed on moonlit nights, the moon penetrating its wide windows. From the center of the veranda a stone stairway descended to the courtyard.

Helena was already there. Dona Ursula had lent her a riding habit, one she had worn occasionally before the counselor's death. The dress fitted her badly: it was much too large for the slender, girlish figure, but her natural elegance made one forget the accessory of clothing.

"I'm ready!" she called, the moment she saw her brother appear at the top of the stairs. "Let's go!"

"Oh, no, it's not going to be like that!" retorted Estacio. "Don't imagine that you are going to ride at once, today, like the young lady you saw go past on the road yesterday. First you must conquer your fear . . ."

"I don't know what fear is," she interrupted with artless simplicity.

"Really? I would not have thought you to be fearless. Well, I know what fear is."

"Fear? Fear is a predisposition of the nerves; such a predisposition can disappear into thin air. Simple reflection is enough to do away with it. When I was a little girl, they told me stories about spirits from the other world. To the age of ten I could not enter a dark room. One day I asked myself if it was likely that a dead person would return to earth. To ask the question was the same as giving the answer. I washed all such foolishness out of my mind, and today I could enter a cemetery at night. . . . But, no, those who sleep there have a right to no longer hear a single murmur from the living world."

Estacio had reached the bottom step of the stairway. He heard these last words with his eyes fixed on his sister as he leaned against the stone support. "Who taught you such ideas?" he asked.

"They are not ideas, they are feelings. They are not learned; they are there deep within one's heart. Sir Geometry," she continued, capriciously brandishing her whip, "see whether these figures of my invention are found in any of your textbooks, and come ride with me."

With a swift movement she caught up the train of her riding habit and walked ahead. Estacio slowly followed, torn between two different emotions; the affection he felt for his sister and the strange sensation that she aroused in him. When he arrived at the stable door, he saw that two horses had been saddled, the stallion of his morning rides and the mare his aunt sometimes rode.

"What's this?" he said. "For the present we'll only go through some elementary steps, here in the yard."

"Of course," she replied.

A slave standing by brought a tambouret. Estacio drew near Helena, who was stroking the mare's mane with her delicate white hand. "What is her name?" she asked.

"Moema."

"Moema! Why that's a native Indian name, isn't it?"

Estacio nodded. Helena had one foot on the tambouret; she again repeated the mare's name as if reflecting upon it without her brother's perceiving that it was a pretense. Suddenly, when he little expected it, she made a leap and landed on the saddle. The mare arched its neck as if proud of the burden. Estacio looked at his sister, marveling at her agility and the correctness of her movement, and without knowing what to think of it. Helena bent toward him. "Did I do it right?" she asked with a smile.

"Could not have been better; but what amazes me..."

Moema's hooves interrupted his remark. The horse-woman brandished her little whip and her mount went out at a canter into the courtyard. In the first moment, Estacio took a step and put out his hand with the intention of seizing the horse's reins; but the young lady's assurance soon made him aware that she was not doing this for the first time. He stood at a distance, admiring her style and dexterity. After twenty paces Helena turned the rein and came back to her starting place.

"How was it?" she asked. "Do you think I have any aptitude for horsemanship?"

"Silly!"

"What's this? Has she learned already?" cried Dona Ursula, who had come out on the veranda.

"She was fooling us," said Estacio. "Did you see how she can ride?"

"She can do everything," Dona Ursula muttered between her teeth.

Estacio mounted his horse, then looked at his watch. It was half-past seven.

"May I go with you?" asked Helena.

"On one condition," he replied, "that is, that you will be sensible. I don't want any feats of daring; the mare is apparently gentle but it is best not to take chances with her. I can see that you are capable of much more..."

"I promise to go along quietly."

Helena saluted her aunt with a graceful gesture, gave her horse its head, and went along at her brother's side. Once through the gateway, they slowly climbed into the hills. The sky was overcast, the morning cool. Helena rode with perfection; from time to time the mare, spurred by her, went a few paces ahead of Estacio's horse; Estacio reproved his sister, with regret because at the same time that he feared some imprudent act on her part he enjoyed seeing the elegant posture of her slender body and the calm firmness with which she governed her mount.

"Aren't you going to tell me," he asked, "why, when you knew how to ride, you asked me to give you lessons?"

"The reason is plain," she replied. "It was simply for fun, a whim...or rather calculation."

"Calculation?"

"Deep, hideous, diabolical calculation," she continued with a smile. "I had a desire to occasionally ride horseback. I couldn't go alone and so..."

"All you had to do was ask me to go with you."

"No, that would not have been enough; there was a way

to give you greater zest for going out with me, and that was to pretend I did not know how to ride. The momentary idea of your superiority in this matter was enough to inspire you with a determined zeal . . ."

Estacio smiled at her calculation, then turned serious and asked coldly, "Have we ever denied you any pleasure you wished?"

Helena trembled, and also turned serious. "No," she murmured, "my debt has no limits."

These words were uttered from the heart. She looked down, and a veil of sadness blotted the sunshine from her face. Estacio regretted his remark. He understood his sister; he saw that, however innocent his words may have been, they could be taken in bad part and in that case the very least he might be accused of was discourtesy. Estacio prided himself on being the most polite of men. He leaned toward her and broke the silence.

"You are offended," he said, "but I forgive you."

"Forgive me?" she asked, raising her lovely tearful eyes to his.

"I forgive the wrong you did me in supposing me rude and ill-mannered."

They shook hands, and the ride continued in the best mood in the world. Helena gave free rein to her imagination and thought; her discourse expressed now romantic sensibility, now the reflection of a premature experience, and went straight to her brother's heart: he rejoiced at seeing in her the woman he wanted her to be — her thoughtful grace, her kindly wisdom. From time to time they reined in their horses to contemplate the road they had traveled, or to chat about something nearby. Once they happened to be discussing the advantages of wealth.

"The material blessings of fortune," Estacio was saying, "are worth much; they bestow the greatest happiness there can be on this earth, that is, absolute independence. I have never experienced poverty, but I imagine that the worst thing about it is not the want created by certain appetites or desires of a transitory nature, but is rather the spiritual servitude that makes a man subject to other men. Wealth buys even time, which is the most precious and fugitive thing we are blessed with. See that black man over there? In order to cover the same distance we do on horseback, he will have to spend an hour more or so going on foot."

The fellow Estacio had spoken of was sitting in the grass beside the road, peeling an orange while the first of the two mules he was leading looked at him philosophically. The black man paid no attention to the two riders coming toward him. He went on peeling his orange and tossing the bits of rind at the mule's nose; each time, the mule barely responded with a movement of its head, something that appeared to give the man infinite delight. He was a fellow about forty years of age; from the look of him, a slave. His clothes were ragged; the hat on his head had already become a very doubtful color. Nevertheless, his face expressed a plenitude of satisfaction and a serenity of mind come what may.

Helena glanced at the figure her brother had pointed out to her. As they went by him he respectfully took off his hat but continued in the same position and occupation as before.

"You are right," said Helena. "That man will spend much more time on the road than we do. But isn't it a simple question of point of view? Actually, time runs on at the same pace whether we squander it or economize it. The important point is not to do many things in the least amount of time but to do many enjoyable and useful things. The most enjoyable thing for that black man is perhaps this very traveling on foot, which lengthens his day's journey and makes him forget his bondage if he is a slave. It is an hour of pure liberty."

Estacio broke into a laugh. "You ought to have been born . . ."

"A man?"

"A man and a lawyer, with your skill for defending the most doubtful causes. I am even willing to believe that you would find slavery itself a blessing if I should say that it is the worst of human conditions."

"So?" retorted Helena smiling. "I am tempted to oblige you, but I won't. I prefer to admire Moema's head. Look! See how arrogantly she tosses it. *She* doesn't curse her condition of slave; she glories in it. And well she may! If she were not our slave, would she have the pleasure of supporting me and carrying me about? But it is not only arrogance, it is also impatience."

"For what?"

"Impatience to race over this Tijuca road and drink the morning breeze, stretching her muscles and feeling that she is a noble, free creature. But what do you expect, my poor little mare?" she went on, leaning her head close to the animal's ears. "Here beside us is a very cowardly, fearful fellow, who is at one and the same time my brother and my enemy . . ."

"Helena!" interrupted Estacio, "You are thinking of racing off in a gallop!"

"And if I did?"

"I would let you go and never take you with me again. You ride well; but I do not want you to do something reckless. *We* are responsible not only for your happiness but also for your life."

Helena reflected a moment. "You mean," she asked, "that if I had an accident some people would lay the blame at my family's door?"

"Exactly."

"Strange people! It will not happen so . . . . For suppose I should take it into my head to leave this life out of disgust with it or out of caprice, you would be accused of offering me the poisoned cup? There could be no better way of making me avoid death."

"Let's drop gloomy talk and go back to the house."

"So soon?"

"I rarely go beyond this point; and don't imagine that we are still near home."

"I feel as though we had just left. Can't we go on for another five minutes? Yes?"

Estacio consulted his watch. "For just five minutes," he said.

"As far as that house with the blue flag."

In fact, there was about four minutes' distance ahead of them, on the left side of the road, a house of insignificant appearance over whose tiled roof floated a blue banner attached to a pole. Estacio recognized the house but it was the first time he had seen the flag. Helena asked him for an explanation of this appendage.

"Why don't you go over and find out?" he said with a laugh.

Helena let out the mare's rein and advanced a few paces. Estacio spurred his horse and overtook her. "Let's not do anything foolish!" he said in a tone of mild remonstrance. "It's some fancy of whoever lives there, or a bird warning, or some other thing not worth the trouble of a silly prank. Let's contemplate the morning, which is delightful."

Helena did not heed her brother's proposal and kept on at a slow pace in the direction of the house. It was an old cottage entered through a door under an old-fashioned penthouse that ran along its front. The penthouse columns were cracked in many places, revealing their brick skeletons. The door was half open, the place deserted, at least apparently. As they came abreast of it, the door opened; but if somebody was watching there he was swallowed up in the shadows, for no one was visible to those outside.

About ten yards further on, Estacio decided they really should go back, and Helena offered no objection. They turned their horses' reins and began to descend.

"Mayn't I speak to the flag?" she asked. "Let me at least

say goodbye." She had already taken her fine cambric handkerchief out of her pocket; she waved it in the direction of the house. Chance decreed that the flag, till then motionless, should move in the breath of a passing breeze. "See how it answered me? Nothing could be more courteous!" she laughed.

Estacio laughed too at his sister's whimsy, and they both descended the mountain, slowly, as they had ascended it. Helena was taciturn and pensive. Her eyes, fixed on Moema's ears, did not appear to see even what path the animal followed. Estacio, to draw her out of her silence, made an observation about something that happened along the way. Helena responded absently.

"What's the matter?" he asked.

"Nothing," she answered. "I was . . . I was intent, listening to that song. Don't you hear it?"

A few yards further on, one heard it distinctly, a song of the fields, half joyful, half mournful. The singer came into view as soon as they rounded a curve in the road. It was the black man they had seen sitting on the ground a short while before.

"What did I tell you?" observed Estacio's sister. "There goes the 'unhappy' man of a short time ago. One orange munched on the grass plus three or four stanzas of song is enough to shorten his journey. You may be sure he goes joyfully on his way and has no need to buy time. Could we say the same?"

"Why not?"

She again withdrew into silence.

"Helena, what you just said . . . Come, we are alone; confess, you have some deep sorrow."

"No, none," she replied. "But I do have a favor to ask of you."

"Name it."

"I beg you to inform me of all the bad impressions of me you may get. Some I will explain, others I will try to dispel by correcting my ways. Above all, I beg you to imprint this truth on your mind and heart: that I am a poor soul flung about in a whirlwind."

Estacio was going to ask for an explanation of those last words; but Helena, as if she anticipated his request, brandished her whip and put the mare in a gallop. Estacio did the same with his horse. A few minutes later they entered the chácara: he, puzzled and curious, she with scarlet cheeks and her heart pounding.

## *Chapter VII*

They dismounted in the courtyard and moved toward the stairway leading to the veranda. His foot on the first step, Estacio said, "Helena, tell me, what did you mean by that remark of yours a few minutes ago?"

"What remark?"

As Estacio shrugged his shoulders with a dejected air, Helena added, "Forgive me. Your request has not, and could not have, any other response but a simple refusal. I will say no more. One should never make half-confessions; but, in this case, complete confession would be a greater imprudence. If it were a question of facts, believe me, there is no one I would rather confide in than you; but why trouble you with the narration of my feelings when I myself cannot understand them?"

Estacio did not insist. They climbed the stairs, crossed the veranda, and entered the dining room, where they found Dona Ursula giving two slaves the orders for the day. Estacio remained thoughtful. Helena's mood and manners changed completely. A few moments before, the melancholy that darkened her face was sincere. Now her customary cheerfulness had returned. One would have said that her spirit was a kind of actress that had received from nature or from fortune, or perhaps from both, a role that obliged her to keep changing costume. Dona Ursula saw her enter all smiles and come give her the usual *good morning,* which was always a kiss, or rather two, one on the hand, the other on her cheek.

"Am I very late?" she asked, whirling round to see the clock on the other side of the room. "Nine o'clock! What a ride, my lord brother!"

Estacio gazed at her in silence and made no reply. Immediately thereafter they went to change, and breakfast brought the family together again. As they breakfasted, Dona Ursula proposed some changes in the arrangement of the chácara, which were discussed at length with her nephew and finally accepted by him. The day was overcast and cool; Dona Ursula went down to the chácara with Estacio. The alterations continued to be studied and put together on the terrain itself with the assistance of the overseer. After the deliberation ended and Dona Ursula's project was definitely agreed upon, Estacio detained her, saying, "I would like a word with you."

"And I with you."

"What are your present feelings in relation to Helena? Oh! there is no need to shake your head or make that weary gesture of annoyance. Judging only from appearances, I do not believe you are totally her friend; but you cannot deny that your antipathy has disappeared, or greatly diminished."

"Diminished, perhaps."

"And with reason. Do you think I did not have some feelings of reluctance when she came here? I did; but if they had not completely disappeared before, they did so this morning."

"How so?"

Estacio related the scene described in the last chapter

and the words Helena had spoken. Dona Ursula smiled ironically.

"You are not impressed?"

"No," she replied decisively. "Helena's remark may be found in one of the many books she reads. Helena is no fool; she wants to attach us in every way, even through pity. I do not deny that I am beginning to be fond of her: she is dedicated, affectionate, diligent; she has refined manners and some social graces. Besides, she is friendly and winsome by nature. Yes, I am beginning to be fond of her but it is an affection without warmth or passion, in which there enters a large dose of habit and necessity. The presence of another woman in this house is convenient because I am tired. Helena fills the need. If, however, anything could injure her in my sight it is that very remark of hers."

Estacio warmly took up his sister's defense. "What I related to you was nothing more than her words. I did not reproduce, nor could I, the sincere manner in which she uttered them, and the depth of sadness in her eyes. I do not deny I felt a slight jolt, and a twinge of doubt, on seeing her change so quickly and enter the room light-heartedly; but it soon passed. She has the ability to bury her afflictions deep in her heart; sorrow also can be hypocritical . . ."

"But what sorrow? what affliction?" interposed Dona Ursula. "The sorrow of being legitimized? the affliction of an inheritance?"

Estacio warmly protested the direction his aunt was giving his ideas. Finally he begged her to cautiously sound out his sister. "A man," he said in conclusion, "is less suited to obtaining a confession of this sort; a lady, respected and a relative, is in a better position to win her confidence and learn the whole truth. Will you undertake this delicate task?"

"You are asking a great deal," replied Dona Ursula.

"Let's see if I accomplish the half of it. Is that all you had to say?"

"That's all."

"Mere child's play! I have something more serious to discuss. Dr. Camargo has written me, a question of..."

"You need say no more," interrupted Estacio. "Here he comes."

Indeed, Camargo appeared not twenty paces away.

"Doctor," said Dona Ursula as soon as he drew near, "you come too soon. I've scarcely had time to frighten my nephew out of his wits with your proposal; he doesn't yet know what you have in mind for him."

"He will presently; all that is needed, Dona Ursula, is for you to tell him you back me."

"I do, completely.

"It is a question of..." said Estacio.

"A conspiracy; we are all conspiring for your good."

Dona Ursula left them to go back into the house. Once the two men were alone, Camargo placed his hand on Estacio's shoulder and gazed at him in a fatherly manner. Finally he asked him if he would like to be a member of the Chamber of Deputies. Estacio could not repress a gesture of surprise.

"That was the question?" he asked.

"I don't think you would call it a question of capital punishment. A seat in the Chamber of Deputies! It's not the same as a cell in the Aljube..."

"But why..."

"The idea has been pestering me for some time. It pains me to see you passively spending your finest years in relative obscurity. Politics is the best career for a man in your circumstances: you have education, strength of character, wealth; you can climb to enviable heights. Recognizing this, I determined to put you in jail...in the Old Jail.[7]

[7]The Old Jail (A Cadeia Velha) was at this time the seat of the Federal Chamber of Deputies.

There is talk of a dissolution of parliament. To assure your victory, I have come to an understanding with the two men who control the votes. It looks to me as if our business is in a fair way to succeed."

Estacio heard him with displeasure. "But, doctor," said he after a brief silence, "you have been somewhat precipitate. The way you have arranged things frees me, so to speak, from any obligation to thank you for your intention. As for accepting, I do not accept."

Camargo was not diverted from his purpose. He let the first wave of disapproval pass over his head, rose out of it, and serenely insisted: "Let us look at things with the eyes of common sense. In the first place, I do not believe you have other projects in mind . . ."

"And if I do?"

"I doubt that they would be more fruitful than this one. Science is arduous and its results make less stir in the world. You do not have an inclination toward commerce or industry. Do your thoughts run on building a suspension bridge between the City and Nictheroy, a railroad into the Matto Grosso, a steamship line to China? I doubt it. Your future is at present bounded by two goals: some scientific studies and the rents from the houses you possess. Well, the election will neither deprive you of your rents nor hinder your research; it will complete you by giving you the public life you lack. The only objection would be a want of political opinions; but this objection will not hold. You must have thought, at one time or another, about the problems of the nation, and . . ."

"Suppose—it is only a hypothesis—that I have some commitments to the opposition."

"In that event, I still say that, even so, you should enter the Chamber, though by the back door. If you hold specific partisan opinions, the prime necessity is to obtain a medium for expressing and defending them. The party that gives you a leg up—if it is not your own, will be consoled by the idea of having helped a talented and honorable adversary. But the truth is that you have not yet made a choice between the two parties; you do not have fixed opinions. No matter! A great number of young men in politics profess, not an opinion that they have examined, weighed, and carefully selected, but the opinion held by their immediate circle, the opinion that their fathers or close friends honor and defend, an opinion that circumstances impose on them. This is the reason for later legitimate conversions to other faiths. Late or soon a man's nature dominates the circumstance of an opinion's origin, and the liberal bud or the conservative bud bursts into a magnificent conservative or liberal lily. Besides, politics is a practical science; I distrust theories that are only theories. Enter the Chamber of Deputies; experience and the study of men and events will show you on which side you belong."

Estacio listened attentively to these utterances with which the serpent directed him to the tree of the science of good and evil. Less curious than Eve, he entered into a philosophical discussion with the reptile. "One enters politics," said he, "out of genuine inclination, noble ambition, interest, vanity, or even for simple amusement. None of these motives impels me to double the Cape of Storms . . ."

"Of Good Hope," corrected Camargo with a laugh; "you can't do away with three centuries of navigation."

Estacio also laughed. Then he spoke to the doctor about his temperament and his ambitions. He did not deny that he had ambition but it was not exclusively of a political nature, nor were all his aspirations of the same dimension. The human spirit, he said, is born a condor or a swallow, or of some other, intermediary species. Some natures demand the vast horizon and the high mountain from whose peak they beat their wings and soar aloft to face the sun. Others are content with a few feet of gliding space and a roof tile in which to hide their nest. These would be the obscure, and, in his opinion, the happy ones. They are not seduced by distant views nor subjugated to the will of other men, they are not mentioned on history's shining pages, nor on its dark pages; the hollow of the tile in which they shelter their young, the tree on which they alight—only these are brief witness to their few days of happiness. When death gathers them in, they will alight on the common bosom of eternity and sleep the same everlasting sleep as the leader who climbed to his high post over a stairway of dead men, the same sleep as the goatherd who once saw him pass and forgot him two hours later. *His* ambitions were not so mean as the goatherd's; they were those of an owner of the land that the leader ravaged. A comfortable income, family, a few books and friends—his boldest dreams went no further.

A pitying smile was the doctor's initial response. "My dear Estacio," he then said, "this mishmash of swallows and goatherds is the most extraordinary thing I could ever hope to hear from a mathematician. Let me tell you, I detest in equal proportion obscure philosophies and poets' rhetoric. Furthermore, when I speak in prose I like people to answer me in prose."

"Did I seem to you to be poetizing?" laughed Estacio.

"Outrageously. Look, I am speaking of serious matters; one must not confound cabbages, the practical part of life, with lilies of the valley, which are the ideological and use-less part."

"So I'm an ideologist."

"You have no right to be."

"Come, leave me to my mathematics, my flowers, and my hunting rifles."

"No! You must mix into all that a dash of politics."

Familiarly taking hold of his coat lapel, Camargo made him sit down with him on a nearby bench. Then he began to speak. This new discourse was the longest he had ever made in all his days. None of the advantages of public life did he neglect to point to with the oily gentleness of the tempter; all its glories, pomps, and satisfactions, not only the real ones but also the fictitious or doubtful were inventoried, colored, gilded, and presented in illuminated capitals. The speech revealed a power of evocation, a vehemence, an energy that no one could have imagined was in him. The man of few words blossomed into a garrulous chatterbox. To speak at such length and with such force, he must have been animated by strong feeling or by some strong personal interest.

Estacio, flattered by the affection he showed for him, had no call to make this last observation. He did not even have the courage to repeat his refusal; he judged it best to postpone his answer to another occasion.

"I have already told you my feelings in this matter. Nevertheless, I am prepared to reflect, and consult Father Melchior and Helena."

Helena's name produced a wry face in Camargo's interior. His exterior reaction did not pass beyond a sly, sardonic smile. There ensued a pause for a pinch of snuff, which he slowly inserted, having extracted it from a tortoiseshell box, a present from Counselor Valle. "Helena!" said he with some hesitation. "How does your sister enter into this business?"

"She is a voice," retorted Estacio, "and a less unimportant one than you think. She has within her a great depth of reflectiveness, a strong, clear reasoning power, in perfect harmony with her other, feminine qualities."

A deep wrinkle shot between Camargo's eyebrows, expressing his alarm and irritation. Estacio's reply had revealed to him a new situation in the family: Helena's opinion, now merely advisory, might come to be preponderant. Such an outcome, which, perhaps, might make the counselor's cold bones shake with joy, had not been foreseen by the medical man. He limited himself to privately taking note of it, and abruptly terminating the conversation said: "Consult anyone you please. Whoever is not of my opinion

is no friend of yours. In any event, no one can say that it is
not friendship, longstanding friendship . . ."

Estacio cut him short by affectionately grasping his
hand. They had risen from the bench. It was almost midday. Camargo hurried off to visit a couple of patients on
the Tijuca road. The counselor's son made his solitary way
through the chácara, deep in thought and troubled. Politics, in his opinion, was an importunate bride; but, if
everyone was conspiring in her favor, would he not be
obliged to marry her? His question was answered by Father
Melchior's voice from a window high above him.

"Come hither, honorable deputy. When are we to hear
your maiden speech?"

## Chapter VIII

Dona Ursula had already told their chaplain of Camargo's
proposal. When consulted by Estacio, the priest replied,
"Weigh your own strengths against the responsibilities of
the office and make your decision."

"I have already decided," said Estacio. "I asked your
advice to bolster my own decision. Isn't that the fate of all
advice? I decided not to accept the candidacy. The political life is too turbulent for my temperament. I am ready
and eager for action but it shall not be out in the world of
men. Given my turn of mind, what would I seek to gain in
the Chamber of Deputies beyond a few prerogatives and a
subordinate role? I would be willing to enter politics only if
I could officiate; but to be merely a sacristan . . ."

"Between the officiant and the sacristan," observed Melchior, "is the predicant: his is a noble and influential post."

"But the text of the sermon, my learned father?" retorted Estacio with a laugh. "I lack the text."

Dona Ursula, seduced by the high position and public stir in favor of her nephew, saw in his reasons pretense or immaturity. She defended Camargo's cause to the best of her ability; she urged her nephew to give it mature consideration before making a definite response. Estacio promised to do so, just as he had promised the doctor, out of simple acquiescence and also to put an end to the subject and go learn the reason for the almost imperceptible smile that grazed Helena's lips. She had left her chair and gone to one of the windows; Estacio joined her.

"I surmised from your smile," said he, "that all this seems puerile to you and that I do well in not accepting what has been offered me."

Helena looked at him in startled amazement but answered calmly, "On the contrary, I think you ought to accept. Besides having my aunt's approval it seems to be the profound wish of Eugenia's father."

It was the first time Helena had alluded to Estacio's love, and she did it in a covert, indirect manner. Estacio, strangely enough, evaded the law of all lovers' hearts: he ignored the allusion and gravely discussed the matter of the candidacy. It was too weighty a subject for a feminine head; Helena interrupted with an observation on two little birds that were dancing together in the air. Estacio accepted the diversion, leaving the electors in peace.

During the next two days, he did not go out of the house. Having received some new books, he spent part of the time leafing through them, reading a page here and there, placing them on their shelves, altering the order and arrangement of the ones that were there, with the bibliophile's loving prolixity. Helena aided him in this work, which was a little like Penelope's, because the order established at noon was sometimes altered at two o'clock, and restored the next morning. Estacio's attention, meanwhile, was not entirely given over to the books. He marveled at his sister's solicitude, at the orderliness and care with which she assisted him. She seemed not to walk but to silently glide from one part of the room to the other, obeying her brother's directions, or trying out an idea of her own. Estacio stopped now and then from weariness; but Helena, unperturbed, went on with her job. If he made some remark about it she answered with a shrug or a smile and continued as before. Then Estacio would grasp her wrists and laughingly exclaim, "Light somewhere, butterfly."

Helena would stop, but only for a few minutes, then she would return to her work with the same serene business of going back and forth. In this way the hours passed in sweet intimacy, and reciprocated affection began to shut out all concern for others. In this way Helena's influence began to assume the proportions of a "preponderant" vote.

On the third day, Dona Thomazia and Eugenia came to dine in Andarahy. Eugenia was that day more sensible and docile than she had ever been; one would have said that she was wearing a disposition as new as the dress she had on, but one less frilly and beribboned. Estacio experienced a sense of satisfaction: the real coincided with the ideal. They were able to speak together alone more than once; it was as if all the members of the household were conspiring to let them have privacy. She was the one who mentioned the political offer; she had chanced to learn of it from overhearing her father's account to Dona Thomazia. Eugenia's wish was for the affirmative; and Estacio, fearful of awakening her slumbering caprices, put up a weak resistance and consented, even more weakly, to reconsider the matter.

"Deputy!" she exclaimed with eyes raised heavenward.

Estacio accompanied Eugenia and Dona Thomazia in the carriage that took them home. The day had been a more or less happy one; the trip back to Rio Comprido was jolly and full of pleasant chat, like a return from a religious festival. The horses appeared to be as lively as the people in the carriage, and shortened the trip several minutes, much to Eugenia's disgust.

Estacio returned to Andarahy in a mood free from all the bad impressions that visits to the Camargo house usually left with him. There had been no disagreement the whole day. Eugenia seemed different, more composed and reasonable. His mood was broken, however, when he entered the house and received the unpleasant news that his aunt had felt unwell soon after he left and had gone to her room. He was alarmed but Helena soon appeared and calmed him, saying that Dona Ursula had only had a bad headache and already felt somewhat better after taking a household remedy.

The next morning, after being informed that his aunt was sleeping quietly, he opened one of his bedroom windows, glanced out over the chácara, and saw Helena standing a few feet away between two orange trees. She was attentively reading something—a long letter written on four sides of paper. Could it be a love letter? The thought troubled him. He moved away from the window, closed the curtains; but, through the gap between them, continued to watch his sister. She was standing in the same place, running her eyes rapidly over the lines of writing till she reached the end of the last page. She took a couple of steps, then stood still and returned to the beginning of the letter to read it again, not hastily, but slowly, lingeringly.

Estacio felt an overpowering curiosity in which there was mixed a black trace of resentment and jealousy. The thought that Helena could share her heart with another saddened and at the same time irritated him. The reason for such possessiveness was a mystery which he did not even attempt to understand; he only knew he felt it, and he stood there without knowing what to do. Twice he turned from the window with the intention of going to his sister but drew back both times, reflecting that his curiosity would appear rude if not tyrannical. After several minutes' hesitation he went out of the room and started for the chácara.

Arrived there, he found Helena pacing slowly back and forth with her eyes on the ground.

"My lady has already gone out!" he exclaimed in a playful tone.

Helena had the letter in her left hand; instinctively she crumpled it as if to conceal it. The gesture did not escape Estacio, who asked with a laugh if it was a counterfeit banknote.

"No, a genuine one," she replied, calmly smoothing the paper and refolding it in its original creases. "It is a letter."

"Young lady's secrets?"

"Want to read it?" she asked, holding it out to him.

Estacio turned red and made a gesture of refusal. Helena slowly doubled it and put it in the pocket of her dress. Innocence never had a fairer countenance; hypocrisy could not have found a more impassive mask. Estacio contemplated her, at once ashamed and suspicious; the letter piqued him, made his flesh tingle. He longed to have the eye of Providence, which penetrates the innermost folds of the heart. Meanwhile they came to tell Helena that Dona Ursula was asking for her. Left alone, Estacio gave himself up to a mental inquiry into the source of the mysterious missive. One indication that it might contain something secret was the gesture with which she had tried to conceal it. But might it not have been from one of her former schoolmates who was confiding *her* secrets to Helena? Estacio embraced this hypothesis with enthusiasm. Then it occurred to him that, even though it was from such a friend, the letter might treat of some boarding school idyll in which Helena had been a protagonist, a living or a dead idyll, a page of hope or of regret. Even so, what had he to do with it?

With this reflection Estacio dismissed the matter from his mind and went to examine improvements that were being made on the chácara, among them a vast cistern. The men were already there, about to begin the day's work. Estacio looked at the work that had been done and gave various new directions. Some were contrary to the plan agreed upon. When this was called to his attention he changed them back again. Next he expressed surprise at not seeing a flower pot that he had ordered removed two days before. Finally he recommended the watering of a plant that was still damp with water the overseer had poured on it that very morning.

Though Dona Ursula did not feel completely well, she was able to sit down to breakfast at the family table. Her nephew appeared irritable, her niece sad. The conversation was repetitiously masticated like the breakfast.

Shortly thereafter, Estacio received a letter from Eugenia. It was a chatty epistle, half frivolous, half sentimental, a mixture of laughs and sighs, with no definite purpose except to beg him to write if he could not come see her. As he finished reading it Helena appeared at the door of his study. He did not hide the letter; he intentionally showed it to his sister in the hope that she would repay him with a like confidence and show him hers.

Helena ran her eyes over Eugenia's letter and for a time remained silent.

"May I give you a word of advice?" she asked.

Estacio responded with a gesture of assent.

"Go see Eugenia, ask her permission to make the formal demand of her father, and conclude this matter now. You love each other, don't you? In her case, I believe I can assert that it is so. As for you . . ."

"As for me?"

"I think it is more doubtful, or you are more secretive. It must be that! You probably consider it a weakness to be in love, although it is the most natural thing in the world, the most beautiful, not to say the most sublime. Serious men have extravagant preconceptions. Confess that you are in love, that you are not indifferent to that inexpressible feeling that binds two human beings together—forever, or for a time."

"Or for a time!" Estacio repeated mentally. And those four words, so natural, so common, had the air of a fresh revelation of the state of mind in which he found himself. If it had been Helena's purpose to throw confusion into his soul, she could not have employed a more effective expression. Could it really be true that this love, so beset with discouragement, disagreements, and changes of feeling, so debated in his own heart, was destined to perish with the honeymoon?

"Yes," he agreed after a few moments, "it is true. Eugenia is not a matter of indifference to me, but can I be sure of *her* feelings toward me? Can she herself make a firm assertion about them? There is much frivolity in her, and it frightens me. She is perhaps deluded by a passing fancy."

"It may be, but it is the husband's task to fix that passing fancy... Marriage is not a solution, I believe; it is a point of departure. The husband will make the wife. I admit that Eugenia does not have all the qualities you might wish; but one cannot ask for everything; one has to sacrifice something, and from reciprocal sacrifice is born domestic happiness."

These observations were just. For that reason, Estacio interrupted them. He found himself in a difficult position. He had walked toward marriage with his eyes closed. On opening them he found himself on the edge of what appeared to him to be an abyss, and it was only a narrow ditch. With one leap he could cross it; but, though he was not irresolute or weak, still, did he have the will to make that leap?

Helena insisting, he promised to go see Camargo that afternoon. But, in the afternoon, a violent thunderstorm broke. And, although the wind and thunder diminished, the rain continued to fall with the same violence. It was impossible to go to Rio Comprido. Estacio rejoiced at the obstacle; it was better to adore the lady's image from a distance than go pluck disappointment in her presence.

Standing at a window in the drawing room he watched

the great sheets of water slide past. Helena sat nearby, not cheerful like him, but taciturn and melancholy.

"It's so good to see it rain when we are under shelter!" he exclaimed. "I have a Latin poet over there in the bookcase who says something of the sort . . . What's the matter?"

"I was thinking of those who have no shelter against the storm, or only a poor one, who do not have a dry roof over their heads nor friendly hearts near them."

Her voice trembled, and tears welled in her eyes so suddenly that she had no time to hide them. Surprised in this display of sensibility, which perhaps puzzled her brother, she rose and started to joke and laugh. The laugh had the sound of tears turned to crystal and the joke was like a response at church. Estacio had not been mistaken; none of this was clear, or . . . was as clear as the letter. His glance, cold and severe, mutely questioned her. Helena, who had had time to calm herself, turned her face toward the street outside the window and began to drum her fingers against the window pane.

## Chapter IX

During the night, Dona Ursula, who had not mended completely, became truly ill. The family, scarcely recovered from the loss of its former head, now found itself threatened by a fresh sorrow, or, at least, subjected to fresh fears. Dr. Camargo pronounced the case serious and started a rigorous treatment.

Under the circumstances, Helena was the logical one to be her nurse. For the first time her filial devotion appeared in all its splendor. She passed the hours of the day and not a few entire nights in Dona Ursula's room, mindful of all the precautions demanded by the patient's grave condition. The medicines and the little nourishment she could take were given her by no other hands. Helena watched at her bed's head during her periods of light, broken slumber, finding in her own strength the resistance that nature reserves especially for mothers. When she allowed her body a little rest it was neither uninterrupted nor of long duration; and more than once in the night she rose from her bed, which had been placed temporarily in the adjoining room, to go look in on the mucama who watched in her place. It was Helena who received the doctor's orders and saw them fulfilled. The cold, hard tone in which Camargo spoke to her was not one to make him more lovable and dear to her but Helena closed her ears to dislike of the man and heard only the physician. *He* had no one else to interrogate concerning the changes in the patient's condition, nor could he have found a better person to observe and report them. Thus, those two who repelled and detested each other pulled together in harmony when the life of a third was in question.

The thing that completed Helena's character and earned her further respect from them all was that, in the midst of her occupations and preoccupations during those days, the regular household discipline did not suffer for an instant. She ruled over the house and servants and served the sick woman with equal watchfulness and kindness. The usual routine, outside Dona Ursula's bedroom, was not altered or disturbed: everything went along in the same way as before, as if nothing out of the ordinary had occurred. Helena knew how to share her attention without dissipating it.

She paid little heed to her own person. Her dress was simple. Her hair, hastily caught up and fixed on top of her head with a comb, did not in all that time receive the elegant and charming look she knew how to give it. Add her dejection of spirits, impossible to avoid with such fatigue, a certain weariness in the eyes that softened them and perhaps made them more adorable, a countenance without smiles or animation, and a silent air of attentiveness and toil.

The illness lasted almost twenty days. In the end, Dona Ursula's constitution, robust in spite of her years, won out. Convalescence began, and with it contentment returned to the household. Helena's role had not ended; it diminished, however, and Estacio intervened to insist that his sister finally take a few days of complete rest. She replied, saying that rest lost little by little would be regained little by little.

There was a wellspring of tenderness in Dona Ursula's heart which Helena had merely to touch to start its free, impetuous flow. The girl's dedication during the crisis was a rod of Moses on that desert of Horebe. The aunt's affection previously had been fainthearted, calculated, and deliberate. After the illness it took on a spontaneous cast. Her experience of Helena's character had caused this as an inevitable result. All her prejudice dropped away; gratitude for her life bound tightly together what so many, earlier circumstances had seemed to keep apart. She did not hide the fact that there had been a change; there was no longer reticence or reserve; her words rose from her heart to her lips without thought, without attenuation; she became tender and motherly.

The day she was able to leave her room for the first time, Helena gave her her arm and guided her to the sewing room, where the family was accustomed to gather in private. Estacio supported her on the other side. Arrived there, they seated her in a comfortable easy chair. Estacio opened the window a little to let in the light and a bit of air. Dona Ursula took a deep breath as if to wash her lungs clean with that first wave of life. Then grasping Helena's hands she pulled her down to her and implanted a long kiss on her forehead as if she were really her mother. Estacio, who stood nearby, was filled with joy at the sight.

"A well-deserved kiss!" he exclaimed. "Helena has been an angel during all this time."

"I am well aware of it," retorted Dona Ursula, "truly an angel, she has been wife, mother, and daughter. Thank you, Helena. It is possible that the medicine helped the cure, but the principal merit is yours alone."

Helena hugged her.

"Estacio," said his aunt, "thank your sister as I have done."

Estacio leaned down in order to place on Helena's forehead a brother's chaste kiss. He did not succeed in doing so, for Helena, turning aside her face, held out her left hand to him with a smile and said, "It was not a service to deserve so great a payment, a handshake and the affection of you both is enough."

Estacio took her hand and felt it tremble. Her gesture of modesty did not seem exaggerated to him or unbecoming. In his eyes, she only appeared the more beautiful for it. A young woman who thought so little of herself as not to admit even a brother's caress—was she not worthy of the family's name?

Dona Ursula's convalescence was slow, and no less surrounded with watchful attentions. The niece and nephew never left her alone for an instant; they invented all sorts of amusements to distract her: games or reading, music, or simple conversation among the three. Once they undertook to present for her alone a comedy acted by two. Another time Helena organized a musical evening in which Eugenia Camargo and three young ladies of the neighborhood took part. It was the first time they had heard Helena sing. Her success could not have been more complete. As the applause she received seemed to make the doctor's daughter somewhat unhappy, Helena deftly arranged a triumph for *her* by asking her to execute a brilliant composition on the piano—her favorite piece. Estacio, who had scarcely taken his eyes off his sister, saw her intention and hinted as much to her. Helena evaded the hint but when he insisted, said, "It was perfectly natural. Eugenia plays beautifully; it was right that she too be applauded. If what

I did was artful it was most innocent art. The best way of living in peace is to foster the amour-propre of others by giving them pieces of our own. But, look, Eugenia does not need even this; she is a princess of beauties. Where will you find a prettier creature?"

Estacio turned his eyes in the direction indicated by Helena, where he saw a group of two young ladies and two young men. Eugenia, on the arm of one of the men, stood listening, without attending, to the conversation going on among them, for her restless eyes spilled over herself and out into the room. She admired herself and was watching to catch the admiration of the others. Her person was truly charming; but Estacio would have liked it to be more unconscious, less preoccupied with the effect it was creating.

"There are a hundred beauties like that one," said he.

"Estacio!" exclaimed Helena in a reproachful tone.

"Beauty is like courage; it is worth more if it is not thrust under your nose."

"You are an ingrate."

That evening the importance won by Helena became more evident than ever; she had become the true mistress of the house, heard and obeyed by all. Dona Ursula had yielded, in a few weeks, what she had refused to grant during many months.

For what reason, then, all things considered, had she not been able to hasten Estacio's marriage? He continued to hesitate, draw back, postpone, and beg for time to reflect. He now paid fewer visits to Rio Comprido; his days, almost all of them, were whiled away in the quiet bosom of the family. But Helena insisted so much that he promised to make the formal demand on New Year's day.

He had not forgotten the letter he saw his sister reading; nevertheless, however much he might watch and observe her he discovered nothing to make him think there was a secret love. None of the men who frequented their house—and there were only a few—seemed to receive from Helena more than common courtesy. Dona Ursula, whom he had engaged to question his sister about the strange thing she said to him on the morning of their first ride, did not succeed in obtaining a more definite response than he had.

His promise to ask for Eugenia's hand in marriage was made the second week in December, on a night when there were no visitors, which were the best nights in his opinion. The following morning he rose late and learned that Helena had gone out for a ride.

"Alone?"

"With Vicente."

Vicente was the slave who, as we already know, became attached to Helena at once, before all the others, and was assigned by Estacio to serve her. The news of the horseback ride displeased him. Although the time passed at its usual pace, his anxiety made it seem longer. He kept going to the window, even down to the chácara gate with an air of apparent indifference that deceived everyone, beginning with himself. One of those times, when he came back to the house, he found Dona Ursula up and told her. She smiled calmly.

"What of it?" said she. "Helena went out with Vicente once before and nothing happened."

"But it's not seemly. It can expose her to some slight, some act of disrespect."

"How? The whole neighborhood knows who she is. Besides, Vicente is not so much of a child any more. Stop worrying; she won't be long. What time is it?"

"Eight."

"Ten or fifteen minutes more. I think I hear hoofbeats now . . ."

They left the dining room and went out on the veranda. Helena and her page were entering the courtyard. She jumped from her horse, handed Moema's reins to Vicente, who had just dismounted, and started for the stairs to the veranda. As she placed her foot on the first step she caught sight of her brother and aunt, waved to them and ran up the stairs.

"Already up and about!" she cried, hugging Dona Ursula.

"Yes," her aunt said with a smile, "and all ready to scold you. What was the idea of disappearing like that? It's the second time you have taken it into your head to go riding without that bear of a brother of yours."

"I didn't want to disturb the bear," she answered, turning to Estacio. "I wanted to go for a ride, and Moema did too. Only an hour and a half."

That was a black day for Helena. Estacio passed almost the whole time in his study; on the few occasions when they met, he spoke in monosyllables, at times only by mute signs. In the afternoon, after dinner, Estacio went down to the chácara. It was no longer only Helena's horseback ride that tormented him; added to the ride was the letter. Could it be that his aunt had been right in her early dislike? As he put this question to himself, he heard behind him a quick step and rustling dress.

"Are you angry with me?" Helena asked softly.

At the sound of her voice his anger melted. He turned. Helena was before him with clear, submissive eyes. Estacio reflected a moment. "Angry?" said he.

"It would seem so. You don't talk to me, don't care about me, go about scowling and grim . . . Is it because I went out for a ride this morning?"

"I admit, I didn't much like that."

"Then I'll not ride any more."

"No; you may go riding. But are you sure you don't run a risk going alone with your young page?"

"None, I am sure."

"And if I ask you never to ride without me?"

"I don't know that I could obey. You will not always be able to accompany me. Besides, going with the boy is like being alone; and my mind sometimes likes to trot freely in solitude."

"Thinking over matters of love, no doubt . . ." He fixed questioning eyes upon her.

His sister made no reply; she took his arm and they walked on in silence for some ten minutes. Coming to a wooden bench, Estacio sat down; Helena remained standing in front of him. They looked at each other without uttering a word; but Estacio's lip quivered several times as if hesitating to say something he had in mind. Finally he overcame his reluctance.

"Helena," said he, "you are in love."

She trembled and colored deeply, looked about her in startled alarm, then placed her hands on Estacio's shoulders. Did she reflect upon what she was about to say? It is doubtful; but her voice on that occasion seemed to concentrate within it all the melodies of human speech, as she slowly sighed, "So much! So much! So much!"

Estacio grew white. Helena stepped back and placed a trembling finger on her lips as if to impose silence. Her cheeks aflame, she turned and walked quickly away from her brother. At that moment the bell on the chácara gate was shaken violently and a voice thundered through the chácara:

"Open up! Open up! For a friend from the other world!"

## Chapter X

Estacio went to the gate, opened it, and a young man standing there entered precipitately. It was Mendonça. The two flung themselves into each other's arms. Helena, a few steps away, observed this effusion and had no difficulty in deciding who the newcomer was.

The effusion ceased, or rather interrupted itself in order to repeat itself. When the two young men judged they had been sufficiently hugged, they started toward the house.

Helena, who was a little ahead of them, was presented to Mendonça. Though surprised to learn she was Estacio's sister, he acknowledged the introduction with ceremonious courtesy. And the two friends went on to the house, where they were joined a little later by Helena herself.

Mendonça was the same height as Estacio, but a little heavier: broad shoulders, laughing, open face, a disposition naturally mercurial and exuberant. He was dressed with great nicety, like the true Parisian he was, freshly plucked from the *grand boulevard,* the Café Tortoni, and the Théâtre Vaudeville. His broad, powerful hands were encased in fine straw-colored gloves, and on his fanciful haircut rested a hat of recent manufacture.

Before entering the house, Estacio explained Helena's situation to him, praising her character and breeding, with a view to making him understand the respect and affection due her. Helena sensed this preparatory work of her brother's the moment she entered the room.

Mendonça entertained the family a part of the evening, recounting the best episodes of his trip. He was an agreeable raconteur, spoke with fluency, in picturesque language, had a good memory and certain powers of observation. A jolly, carefree spirit, he was prone to discover the comic side of things, and took more delight in recounting incidents of a hotel dinner or a night at the opera than in describing the beauties of a Swiss landscape or the remains of Rome.

His visit lasted little more than an hour. Estacio offered to accompany him to the city but Mendonça refused to let him go beyond the chácara gate. As they walked through the chácara, they spoke of the past and a little about the future, in disconnected snatches as the place and occasion prompted. When Mendonça saw that Estacio did not touch on one essential subject, he brought it up himself.

"In one of your letters you mentioned a certain Eugenia . . ."

"Camargo's daughter."

"Just so. Business broken off?"

"On the contrary, almost finished."

"Finished . . . ? in church I suppose."

"That's right."

"When?"

"Soon."

"Married at last! It was all you lacked. You were born to be a husband, as I a vagabond; I don't know which of us is on the right path."

"Perhaps we both are."

"Yes, I think so. It all depends on one's taste. Marriage is the worst or the best thing in the world, purely a question of temperament. I saw your young lady a few times; she was then a child. I don't need to ask you if she is an angel . . ."

"She is an angel."

"Like all brides. Lucky Estacio! You follow the career of your choice while I . . ."

"You?"

"I interrupt mine, perhaps forever. I have to think about earning a living; I am not a man of means, no more is my father. Travel, I kiss you goodbye!"

"So much the better! I'll get you a wife. You may not be inclined that way but you will not be the first man to wander from his chosen path without causing inestimable damage to the universe."

"All right, get me a wife, only . . . let it not be your sister."

"Oh, no!" Estacio answered quickly.

"I'll admit, she's nice to look at, but if you will allow me to use our old-time frankness, I detect in her an inbred streak of disdain."

"What an idea! She is the most amiable creature in the world. You will see . . . Today, perhaps, she *was* preoccupied. Anyway you should not have expected her to jump up and dance with you through your wild conversations."

Mendonça finished lighting his cigar, shook hands with Estacio, and went out the gate.

Estacio awoke from a dream. Reality placed its leaden hands on him and repeated in his ear Helena's interrupted confession. Anxious to know the rest, he hastened into the house. To no purpose, because his sister had retired for the night. Estacio followed her example. He must wait a whole night, a delay that distressed him because, as he told himself, it was his duty to watch over Helena's life, both as a brother and as head of the family, to discover her sentiments and arrange what was best for her. One night was not much, still, his preoccupation held off sleep. His sister's sudden confession, brief and eloquent, remained in his mind like the repeated echo of a voice that had died away.

Neither the next day nor on subsequent days did he get what he had hoped. Helena either avoided being alone with him or somehow evaded further explanation. On their morning rides, which were frequent, Estacio sought, more than once, to bring up the subject that occupied his thoughts. Helena would listen with a smile and answer with a jest; then with a touch of the rein she would wheel the conversation about to gallop off in the opposite direction. Since fantasy was a vast territory, Estacio never succeeded in bringing her back to the point of departure.

One day his insistence had such a character of authority that it quite evidently constrained and offended Helena. Her response was a sarcastic remark; he retorted with a harsh rebuke. They were going along on foot, leading their mounts by their reins. On hearing her brother's rude speech, she checked her step and fixed him with a look of proud dignity, one of those looks that seem to come from the stars no matter what the stature of the person may be. Estacio possessed these two attributes of a magnanimous nature: a willingness to admit error and to ask forgiveness. He saw that he had yielded to a mean-spirited impulse and confessed as much, and in such words that Helena reached for his hand and said, "Thank you! If you had not said this to me you would have seen me fly down that road clear to the end of the world or even to the end of life."

"Helena!"

"Oh! it is not a vain sensitivity; it is what my position forces upon me. You can regard my life here with complacent eyes, but, the truth is, only the wings of your favor protect me . . . So, be generous, always, as you were just now. Do not seek to violate my heart's inmost shrine. Do not insist on asking for an explanation of words spoken without thinking in an unlucky moment . . ."

"Without thinking? Perhaps, but for that very reason true. If you had taken time to think, you would have kept them shut up within you, hoarding your secrets and distrusting friendly hearts. My purpose was only to help you to happiness, to undo . . ."

"It is late!" she interrupted, consulting the watch fastened to her belt. "Let's go."

Estacio smiled sadly as he offered her his knee; she placed her slender foot on it and sprang lightly into the saddle. The ride back was less cheerful than it usually was. They talked, but speech came to their lips like a hesitating, muffled wave on the shore; no anger, but no animation. So went that day, so would have gone other days if it were not for Helena's magic wand. Her natural charm was so great that her brother soon forgot his displeasure in the hours passed in her presence—looking at her, listening to her voice—both of them content and satisfied; those were the happiest moments of his day. The episode of the confession sometimes came like an unwelcome guest to project its misty shape between them; but Estacio's mind repelled it and his sister's sunny nature did the rest.

Meanwhile, thanks to his recently arrived friend, the counselor's son decided to depart a little from his habitual routine and began to taste some of the life on the outside.

Mendonça was trying to realize in miniature his evaporated Parisian ideal. He had a constant urge to be on the move, an impulsiveness and love of noisy good fun, which hitherto completely wanting in Estacio now gave *his* life the variety it had lacked. Some plays and promenades, a jolly supper or so, such was the program for this low side of Estacio's existence. To contrast with it he had his mornings in Andarahy and an occasional night in Rio Comprido. He told his friend and his conscience that he was waving good-bye to liberty.

Mendonça's influence extended even into the Valle home. What Mendonça liked was variety in life; he could not endure either the same pleasures or the same cigars; to appreciate them he had to change them frequently. If it had been possible he would have turned monk during the month before Carnival, then doffed the habit for the domino and mingled the last notes of matins with the introductions to the contra-dance. His devotion to fashion was somewhat troublesome for him because fashion did not keep pace with his impatience. In his opinion what distinguished man from beast was the faculty for seeing to it that one night not resemble the next. Rio de Janeiro did not offer the same resources for variety that Paris did, but with an inventive, fertile mind such as his he could not fail to find a way of escaping uniformity in his habits.

The worst thing that could happen to him was the disparity between his desires and his means. Son of a tradesman who could barely make ends meet, he would not have been able to realize the European trip in the grand proportions in which he did, if it had not been for the beneficent intervention of an old lady relative who took it upon herself to supply the resources he lacked, during that long absence from home. Now the lady-relative's purse was no longer open to him and his father was unwilling to foster habits of idleness. He did go to the trouble, however, of obtaining a government job for his son. Mendonça was by no means averse to accepting it; all he asked was that it should not remove him from the capital. Restless, fond of the hub-bub and easy life in the Court City of the Braganças, intelligent without having broad horizons, possessing just enough education to routinely discharge duties of a certain order, Mendonça, with all his defects and good qualities, was an agreeable and acceptable fellow. His defects were rather those of his head than of his heart. The variety he demanded in external things of small importance had no part in his friendships; there, he was unchangeable and loyal. He was capable of sacrifice and dedication, especially if he was not asked to deliberate about the sacrifice or reflect upon his dedication; it had to be a sacrifice demanded by a sudden, unforeseen circumstance.

No wonder if the presence of such a man had the effect of modifying the tone of the society of which Estacio's family was the center, whenever he put in an appearance. He was the sun of that land. He did not have the stiffness of a man of fashion nor the affected foreign mannerisms of a true expatriate. The fashionable cut of his clothes could not disguise his open, expansive nature. Received as a son in that house, he found there a partial home. What better form could life have than in that family bound together by a sentiment of love?

## Chapter XI

New Year's Eve came to muddy those clear waters. Since it was Estacio's birthday, Dona Ursula had decided to invite several people to dinner and several more for the evening — a small intimate party. She and Helena bustled about to make the little family celebration worthy of its object. Estacio was for suppressing the evening party, but it was difficult to get loving hearts to desist from their purpose.

As soon as he was up that morning, and he rose early, Helena asked him to go with her to the sewing room. "I want to give you my present," said she.

As soon as they entered the room, she opened a portfolio in which there was a single drawing, but that one significant. It was a stretch of Andarahy road over which they were accustomed to ride, but with certain particularities of the first day. Two riders, he and she, going up the hill at a leisurely pace; in the distance, above them, could be seen the old house flying the blue flag; in the first plane, the colored man and his mules descending the hill. Beneath the sketch, a date: the 25th of July, 1850.

Estacio could not repress a gesture of admiration when Helena folded back the tissue paper that covered the drawing. He took her hand and held it in his as he examined the work. He noted the strong lines, the exactness of local circumstances—the impressions of a fugitive hour which the art of his sister's pencil had fixed on paper.

"You could not have given me a better present," he said. "You give me a part of yourself, the daughter of your mind and spirit. And what a daughter! There are not many young women who can draw like that. So this was why you went out alone those times with only your page!" He contemplated the sketch some moments longer, then raised it to his lips. The kiss fell on the lady-rider's head. It was the original who colored.

"You two go around boasting of my talents," said Helena after a moment; "I was vain enough to want to give a small sample . . ."

"A superb sample! Don't you think, aunty?" Dona Ursula had appeared in the doorway, bringing her present in a little jeweler's box.

Dona Ursula, it is certain, did not possess a flair for art, but love of family had taught her the heart's aesthetics and these were enough to make her admire Helena's work.

"What have I been saying all along?" she cried. "This child knows how to do everything!"

"Only *almost* everything," Helena corrected. "I do not know, for example, how to thank you for . . ."

"For what, silly?" interposed her aunt. "Some nonsensical thing, no doubt, improper to mention at any time but more especially on a day like today."

While the two ladies went to take care of arrangements for the day, Estacio ordered his horse saddled and went for a ride. He wanted to compare once more Helena's sketch with the scene she had copied. Her fidelity was perfect, and the scene would have been exactly the same as her picture if certain circumstances of that first occasion had been present. Helena was not riding at his side; but there not forty yards distant floated the blue flag over the cottage with the old-fashioned penthouse. Estacio slowed his horse's pace, savoring his recollections of that first morning, when Helena appeared so strangely moved. He again began to reflect on her situation and the passion she had confessed to with such vehemence a few days before. If it could possibly be brought to a happy conclusion, Estacio promised himself, no matter what the difficulties, he would secure that happiness for her. Would that not be serving the blood of his blood?

The little dwelling with the penthouse, up to then a matter of indifference to Estacio, now held a special interest for him. The closer he came to it the more he recognized that it was a faithful reproduction of Helena's sketch. The sketch did not present all the building's particularities of age, but it had the same general appearance and proportions, as if it had been made in the presence of the original.

At one of the windows was a man engrossed in reading, his head bent over the book, which lay on the window sill. In that position it was not easy to get a good look at him; it would appear, however, he was a virile, handsome fellow.

At ten yards' distance, he raised his head and fixed Estacio with a pair of large, serene eyes, then immediately withdrew his gaze, lowering it to the book.

"Little do you know, O matutinal philosopher," said Estacio to himself, "little do you know that your house has been reproduced by the most beautiful hand in the world!"

The philosopher continued to read, the horse to travel. On his way back a few minutes later, Estacio found only the house; its tenant had disappeared, a circumstance of indifference to him, which totally escaped his notice. He gave the incident no more thought. His mind was cantering hard in the English manner, like his jennet, and both drank the wind, anxious to arrive at their point of departure.

## Chapter XII

The night's festivities proceeded at a lively pace although the party was small. Some whirling waltzes, two or three quadrilles, cards, music, much conversation and laughter, such was the program that filled the night's hours and made them short.

If it was Helena who did the honors of the house, the life of the party was Mendonça, whose high spirits had already won him universal suffrage. Eugenia had been the first to cast her vote for him, for there existed between these two an affinity of temperament that attracted them to each other. Mendonça indulged her whims, applauded her, understood her, obeyed her without constraint or remark. When he waltzed with her, all eyes were centered on them. They were both waltzers of the first order. The undulations of Eugenia's body and her serene sureness of foot were marvelously adapted to that sort of dance. It was agreeable to

see the two travel the vast circle opened for their movement, to see them finally stop with the same precision, and
without the least token of weariness. Each time the music
paused, or the waltz ended, Eugenia gave her entire attention to the gesture of her arm with which she gathered the
skirt of her dress close against her body. The pleasure with
which she made the gesture and the graceful way she
accompanied it by a slight inclination of her body showed
that coquettishness rather than necessity moved both hand
and body. Triumphs of that sort filled Eugenia's soul to
overflowing, and since she did not have either the modesty
or the art to disguise it one saw in her face her pride and
satisfaction. Dance was not only a pleasure and a diversion
for Camargo's daughter, it was also an ornament and a
weapon. Naturally the most intrepid and serious waltzer
was her perfect spiritual partner, and no one denied the
tradesman's son that role.

"Your daughter is the queen of the evening," murmured
Dr. Mattos in Camargo's ear during a pause in their game
of ombre.

"She really is, isn't she?" Camargo replied, and his soul
took flight on the fluttering ends of the sash that hugged
his daughter's waist, never returning to its legal residence
except when the dancer stopped in her dancing. Then he
would glance around as if demanding equal admiration
from the others. Afterwards he would turn gloomy and fall
into long, deadly silences. Three or four times he approached Helena without succeeding in detaining her or in
finding in himself more than a couple of trivial phrases. He
persisted, never losing her from sight, apparently anxious
to talk to her about something.

Helena shared herself among all those present, attentive
to the needs of each and to the thousand things the night
required. She sang once, danced a quadrille, but refused
to waltz. Mendonça insisted in vain; she excused herself,
saying it made her dizzy. In the opinion of the colonel

major's son, that reason was only a cover for her ignorance. Estacio thought otherwise, that it was his sister's savage modesty, which would not permit a man's touch, a thought that did his heart good.

Around midnight, after supper was over, the ladies exchanged impressions and comments, the younger men were smoking, the card players settling their scores. Night had not cooled the air; the lively movement and conversation increased its heat. Helena, like Dona Ursula, was worn out; she retired for a few moments to the room adjoining the drawing room. There she sat down on a sofa and leaned back, lightly relaxing her body and letting her eyelids droop, whether in thought or because they were heavy with sleep is difficult to say. Her mind had not had time to frame two ideas or to start a dream when a voice aroused her.

"Already asleep?" It was Camargo.

Helena opened her eyes with a start. His voice produced on her the disagreeable impression it always did. She smiled a forced smile, and, perceiving that he was about to seat himself beside her, deliberately neglected to draw back the skirt of her dress, as if determined to leave a wide space between them. Camargo sat down.

"Did I frighten you?" said he.

"A little."

His hands played with the numerous charms on his watch chain, then he took hold of her fan in a familiar manner, opened it, counted the sticks, and returned it with a compliment. Helena's answer was a smile. She started to get up but he detained her with these words: "I am glad to find you alone, because I need to ask your advice."

Helena's brows drew together in a questioning frown.

"Advice and a favor," the doctor continued. "It will not be the first time, I believe, that age has consulted youth.

Besides, it concerns a matter on which young people speak ex cathedra."

Helena looked at him distrustfully. She had never seen him so affable, and this change of manner and tone frightened her.

It was true; he was going to ask her something. He did not delay. He gave a rapid exposition of his relations with the counselor's family, of the friendship that bound him to them. "Nothing can make up for the loss of my late friend," he added in conclusion, "but there is some compensation in the affection that survives and makes me consider this family mine. I am certain your brother and Dona Ursula feel the same way in respect to me. As for you, you are recent in the family but have no less right to my regard than they. I knew you when you were so small!"

"Knew me?"

Camargo nodded. Helena quickly glanced around the room, fearful that someone had entered and overheard. Once assured that there was no one, she had a contrary reaction: she became ashamed of her fear. Her shame increased when the doctor said in a low voice, "Let's not speak of that . . ."

"On the contrary!" she cried. "You may speak freely. Tell it all. She was my mother. I do not know what she was to other people, but if they have pardoned the irregularity of my birth I do not believe they would ask in exchange the renunciation of a daughter's love. The law that placed it in my heart is before and above men's laws. I do not repudiate a single one of my memories of that other time. I know and comprehend that society has laws and regulations worthy of respect; I accept them as they stand, but let them leave me at least the right to love the dead. My poor mother! I saw her expire in my arms, caught her last breath. I was scarcely twelve years old, yet I did not permit anyone else to watch at her bed's head the last night she passed on earth... Oh! I will never forget her! Never! Never!"

Helena uttered these words in a state of exaltation that no one had ever seen in her before. In vain did Camargo try, several times, to stop her, apprehensive that they would hear in the next room, for she had raised her voice. She did not heed him, did not even see his imploring look. Beneath the modest folds of her dress, her bosom undulated in a stormy sea of passion. Her last word came out a sob. Camargo felt surprise at this explosion of tenderness. It was obvious he had expected something quite different. There followed a brief silence, during which Helena chewed the edge of her handkerchief as if to hold back the tumult of words that thronged her heart.

Finally the doctor went on with his discourse. "No one is asking you to forget her," said he, "everyone has respect for such feelings of filial devotion. The past is gone, and the least that we owe the dead is silence. You have the right to give her your love and grief. But let us speak of the living; and forgive me if I have touched, without wishing to, on such a sorrowful remembrance."

"No! No! It is not sorrowful!" said she, shaking her head.

"Let us speak of the living. Don't you feel certain of your family's love?"

She made a gesture of assent.

"You could not find a better, kinder family. Dona Ursula is a sainted lady; Estacio has a firm, upright character. Let us come now to the matter of advice. For a long time I have been toying with the idea of going to Europe. I am getting on in years and am unwilling to give up the hope of seeing something besides our Pão de Açúcar. I've already postponed the trip more than once. I believe I can now actually realize my hope. There is, however, one problem. You know my daughter loves your brother? *My* eyes long ago discovered their inclination toward each other, for your brother also loves my daughter. They are worthy of each other's affection, and in a sense they continue the affection that existed between their fathers; nature completes nature. This is the situation. What I would like is for you to tell me whether I ought to go now, taking her with me, or if it is better to wait until they marry."

Helena listened without looking at him. When he finished speaking she gazed at him with astonishment and curiosity. The silliness of the question was so obvious that she tried to read in his countenance his real, hidden thought.

Camargo hastened to explain. "Estacio," said he, "may love Eugenia with the idea of marriage in mind; but also it may not go beyond a chapter of romance such as one reads on the ferry between the City and Nictheroy. He is of a serious turn of mind, but the heart has its own special laws. I confess that Estacio's present behavior does not reassure me in this matter. There have been changes in him that are hard to explain. The time that has elapsed is more than sufficient for him to . . . Do you follow me?"

"Yes."

"And . . ."

"I imagine you are asking more of me than you said. You want me to ferret out Estacio's intentions?"

"That's right."

"But why don't you go to him yourself?"

"There is no reason why I couldn't, except that it is an established custom that a father ought not be the first to speak in such affairs. One must respect a father's dignity. Add the fact that Estacio is rich, a circumstance which might cause people to suspect an avaricious motive on my part, though such is far from my thoughts. I *could* speak to Dona Ursula. I am convinced, however, that she does not have your address and . . . why should I not say the word? your influence over Estacio's mind."

"I?"

"Oh! an incontestable influence! Your coming has completed your brother's soul; you are its other half. Besides, in such matters, a sister is a brother's natural confidante and counselor."

Helena gave three little taps on her knee with the tip of her fan and with narrowed eyes glanced at the door communicating with the drawing room, then turned back to the doctor. "I know they love each other," she said, "and I have already expressed my opinion in the matter. Eugenia, it would appear, is my friend; my brother is my brother; I wish them every happiness. There is, however, a limit to a sister's right to intervene; I am unwilling to go beyond that limit. Besides, your request is otiose."

"Why?"

"Announce your intended trip, and Estacio will hasten to ask you for your daughter's hand. If he does not, it is because he does not love her as she deserves, and in that event it is better to lose a marriage than to make a bad one."

"You think so?" asked Camargo.

"Of course."

"Your advice is excellent," he said after a moment, "but it has the substantial defect of eliminating your intervention, and that is necessary to me. Let us see how things would work out. Suppose I announce my trip and Estacio does not respond as I hope. What should I do?"

"Embark."

"But that would endanger the marriage. Look, this marriage . . . is one of my dreams. I want the children to continue the affection that was their fathers'. If Estacio draws back, my hopes vanish like a puff of smoke; time will cut a chasm between them; Eugenia will fall in love with someone else . . . In short, I count on you."

"On me?"

"You have determination, a fund of expedients, a mind equal to delicate undertakings of the sort, and since it is a question of a brother's happiness I believe you will make every effort to bring to fruition this purest of fatherly ambitions. It is not a trifle that I ask of you, it is my daughter's happiness."

Helena made no reply. She looked at him askance, then fastened her gaze on the white eagle woven in the carpet, on which she had set an angry, impatient foot. She might have told him at greater length what her role with Estacio had been in respect to Eugenia: her requests and demands, and her brother's promise which would be fulfilled, if it was to be fulfilled, within a few days. But she refused to raise hopes that events could dissipate. Besides, her heart would not consent to a greater confidence. Both of them were aware that they heartily detested each other; but, if there was suppressed anger within Helena, Camargo was all calm observation. He contemplated her with the fixed, metallic stare of a cat, while the thin, hairy fingers of his left hand beat a tattoo on his knee. He did not speak but his whole being was one imperious question mark.

Helena glanced at him once more. "Will you give me your arm as far as the drawing room?" she asked.

Camargo smiled. "Only that? I was telling myself something different."

"What?"

"I was telling myself that much is to be hoped from the dedication of a young lady who finds a way to visit, at six o'clock in the morning, an old, poor house—not so poor, however, as not to be gallantly decorated with a blue flag..."

Helena became livid; she wildly grasped Camargo's wrist. In her eyes one saw terror, anger, and shame. Through clenched teeth she hissed one word: "Hush!"

"I speak between ourselves and God," he said.

A wave of color spread over her cheeks with the same rapidity they had turned pale. She tried to stand but felt weak. No one perceived her emotion or her gesture. No one was looking that way. Camargo leaned toward her and spoke some lively words of encouragement, which she interrupted, murmuring, "You are cruel!"

"I am a father," he replied, "a fond, provident father, even more provident than fond. I am counting on you."

## *Chapter XIII*

Immediately the party broke up, Helena retired for the night, on the pretext of being ready to drop from weariness, but actually to pay nature her tribute of tears. Repressed despair raged in her heart, threatening to burst out. Helena entered her room, closed the door, uttered a loud cry, and threw herself on the bed, weeping and sobbing.

Beauty in anguish is one of the most pathetic spectacles nature and fortune have to offer for man's contemplation. Helena writhed on her bed as if all the winds of misfortune had been loosed upon her. She vainly tried to choke back her sobs, digging her teeth into the bolster, she moaned, and mingled her tears with cries of disconnected words and phrases. Her hair, which had come down in the violence of her agitation, she coiled around her neck, hoping for death as the handiest remedy. With furious hands she tore open her dress, releasing her young breast from its chaste prison so that it could unburden itself of the sighs that filled it. She wept long, wept all the tears she had spared during those placid, happy months, soul-soothing tears that little by little hushed the cries of her anguish.

Hushed, but not lulled it to sleep; it remained her companion throughout that cruel night: both kept vigil. When her eyes grew tired, and there were longer intervals between the sobs, she lay motionless, her face in the pillow, fleeing the sight of the reality outside. She lay so for an hour, mute, prostrate, as though dead, for a long, long, long hour such as only the clocks of despair and hope tell.

When the force of the storm had spent itself, she sat on her bed and looked vacantly about her. Then she rose and unsteadily directed her steps toward her dressing room. There she stopped before the mirror but immediately turned away as if it were painful for her to face herself. One of the windows was open; she went to it to get a breath of air. The night was clear, tranquil, and hot. The stars scintillated with a liveliness that made them seem joyful. Her eyes threaded their way among them, as if seeking a road to happiness. She remained at the window about half an hour, then turned back inside, sat down, and wrote a letter.

The letter was long, written in a rush of rapid phrases without sequence or order; it contained many complaints and imprecations, expansive tenderness mixed with a profound despair; it spoke of those born under an evil star who have only intermittent, inconstant snatches of happiness; it told how, for her, happiness was a germ of death and dissolution—she repeated this three times as if the observation were a transcript of her actual experiences. The letter spoke also of a man in whom a father's egoism knew no limits, who desired at all costs to marry his daughter to a great fortune and a great position—a "man," she wrote, "who from the very beginning viewed me with hateful eyes because of the diminution I would cause the inheritance." In closing she said there was much that was obscure and incomplete in these lines, that she would tell everything when she had the opportunity but for the present she must give the sad notice that it was imperative that she refrain from going out.

Helena reread what she had written, pondered a long time over it, added a few more lines, then she tore the sheet in two, held the pieces to the candle and destroyed them. As if she repented her act, she began another letter but did not complete six lines; she tore it up as she had the first one, and only then did she have recourse to the best remedy for a lacerated, devout heart; she prayed. Prayer is the mysterious stairway that Jacob dreamed of. On it thoughts ascend to heaven; on it divine consolations descend to earth.

Meanwhile night began to pour its urn of hours into dawn's hands. Sleep had fled Helena's eyes, but it was imperative for her to get some rest. Still dressed, she flung herself on the bed, but not to sleep; it could not be said she slept; she lay there in a state between wakefulness and slumber until daylight came. Opening her eyes she seemed to awaken from a dream; her imagination recomposed all the stages of what had happened the day before. Then she sighed and stared at the floor with the tragic and solemn fixity of death. "It had to be," she murmured from time to time.

She rose, finally, depressed and tired. She looked at herself in the mirror. The lack of color in her face and the purple around her eyes could hardly fail to make an impression on the family. She explained away as best she could those vestiges of the storm, giving a most likely explanation for them as fatigue from the day before and a sleepless night. The explanation was readily accepted by her aunt and brother. Only Father Melchior, when he saw her, fixed her with a doubting look that made her lower her eyes.

If Helena felt poorly, wasn't Estacio's place with her? This was the way *he* reasoned, and he resolved not to leave the house all day. He surrounded her with attentions, tried to distract her, begged her to go rest a bit. To justify the explanation she had given, Helena obeyed her brother's instruction. *He* shut himself up in his study, where he occupied the time going over papers and putting them in order. It was the day set for him to ask Eugenia's hand in marriage, yet he had no thought of going to Rio Comprido. It was his sister he thought about; it was she that filled his thoughts while rereading favorite passages in his books, or sending to inquire if she was sleeping peacefully, or contemplating the sketch she had presented to him the day before. He felt so lucky on that dawn of the new year!

A little before dinner time, he heard the rustle of skirts along the hall, and his sister appeared in the doorway. She looked the same as before, but to Estacio it appeared that rest and sleep had actually restored her well-being. The reason for it was the studied smile that enlivened her countenance. Helena stood there and Estacio went to her, took her hand in his and made her come into the room. "Are you better?" he asked.

"I'm fine."

"Didn't I say it was best to give up the idea of the party? These affairs go on and on and wear one out, especially a person with a delicate constitution..."

Helena shrugged her shoulders.

"Come, sit down a while."

"First, you must answer my question."

"What question?"

"What day is this?"

"New Year's."

"Do you remember what you promised me?"

"Perfectly. You see these papers?" He pointed to the secretary on which lay a neat pile of papers that had been classified and arranged in order. "I have been busy liquidating the past; I still lack some late accounts, which my agent will bring me tomorrow. Afterwards I will go..."

Helena shook her head with an air of disapproval. "No," she said, "there will be no 'going afterwards'; you will go this very day. What have your accounts to do with the authorization you must ask of Eugenia? Go right away, tonight. I am superstitious; I believe that a proposal made on this day will be of good omen; it will bring a lucky year."

"My intention was to go within four or five days," Estacio

replied after a silence, "but I do not hesitate to do it sooner. Once that formality has been complied with..."

"...you will immediately ask her father's consent."

"No!"

"Why not?"

"Because I'll need to think about it another twenty-four hours at least. Twenty-four hours is not much for a man who is about to put himself in chains for eternity. I want to sound my own feelings, and..."

"But all this is utter nonsense!" interposed Helena, seating herself on the edge of the hammock in which Estacio used to lie and read. "Do you expect to back out after declaring yourself to her?"

"Oh, no! But, since I am headed for such a solemn, conclusive act, there is no harm in going slowly, a step at a time. You are surprised?" he asked, for he saw her make a gesture of impatience.

"I am enraged."

"But..."

"You are insufferable. You are breaking your promise."

"I have already said I will keep it."

"You will not back out?"

"No."

"You will go make the marriage proposal this very day?"

"To her."

"To her *and* her father."

"I'll write her father a letter."

"All right, let it be a letter! So long as you make an end of this business. The wedding will take place..."

"When it suits Dr. Camargo."

"Before the end of the month."

"So soon!"

"I give you a month and a half. Not an hour more! I am dying to see you two married, as much for your sake as hers, poor girl! She loves you so much..."

"You think so?" Estacio asked eagerly.

"Yes, I do! I would take my oath upon it. It may not be love as you would wish it but it is the love that she can give you, and it is much... Agreed then! Word of honor?"

Estacio silently held out his hand. Helena grasped it firmly.

"I am about to entrust my destiny to the lightest head in the universe," said Estacio with his eyes on the ground. "It is not her heart that I complain of, it is her mind, which has never outgrown its baby clothes. Besides, as I approach nearer the solemn hour, I feel a repugnance for the conjugal state. My bachelor life is so good! my days so full of..."

Helena stopped his mouth with one hand, with the other she made a sign for him to be silent. Then she abruptly left him. Alone, Estacio reflected for a long time on the situation in which he found himself. He recognized that he was morally obligated to ask Eugenia in marriage, since their hearts, once opened to each other, had as good as sealed a contract that only he could *not* break. His conscience resisted his heart's vacillations; his decision was immediate.

That same night Eugenia heard the hoped-for request. The joy that spilled from her eyes was characteristically beyond measure. A little more modesty would not have been unsuitable to the occasion. There was none; her first act as woman and wife was a childish one. Eugenia was ignorant of everything, including her sex's art of dissimulation. In bestowing her hand upon Estacio she was not the lord of the castle who rewards a knight; she was the knight who receives the reward in a flurry of eager submission.

Now that the Rubicon was crossed, there was nothing for it but to march straight to the eternal city of matrimony. Estacio wrote Dr. Camargo the next day, asking for Eugenia's hand; the letter was cold and formal, as the circumstances demanded. Before sending it he showed it to Helena, but she refused to read it. She did not read it or even take it from his hand. He held it a few moments without the courage to give it to the slave who was waiting for it. Finally he laid it down on the secretary. "Tomorrow," he said to Helena with a smile.

Helena snatched up the letter and gave it to the slave. "Take it to Dr. Camargo's house," she ordered. "There will be no reply."

## Chapter XIV

Camargo was sitting down to dinner when they handed him Estacio's letter. He read it to himself, but his daughter read it in his eyes. A gentle zephyr of heavenly bliss smoothed the wrinkles from the doctor's brow; his lips—it was a terrifying thing!—parted in a broad smile, a smile that ended in a burst of laughter, the first laugh that Dona Thomazia had ever heard come out of him. After dinner Camargo and his wife went into the drawing room, where he told her of the formal request for his consent and the two parents sent for their daughter. On hearing the announcement, Eugenia neither lowered her eyes nor blushed. Asked for her answer, she replied that the marriage was much to her liking.

"Really?" said Camargo in simulated surprise.

Eugenia made a slight inclination of the head with the air of one who would say that she did not believe in her father's surprise. He caught hold of his daughter's hands and pulled her to him.

"So, then, my angel," he said, "you marry of your own free will? Estacio is the chosen of your heart? I laud your choice; you could not have made a more honorable one. You will be the heir of your mother's virtues; I propose her as the best model there is on earth."

"The most conscientious at least," put in Dona Thomazia, content and proud at her husband's praise. "She will be a good wife, modest, thoughtful, and economical."

"Economical but not penurious," added Camargo. "Wealth ought not to be squandered, but it is also true that it imposes unavoidable obligations, and it would be the height of impropriety for us to live beneath our means. You must not do that, nor fall into the opposite extreme; seek a middle term, the position of good sense. Neither wasteful nor miserly."

Dona Thomazia concurred in her husband's explication, while Eugenia, looking from one to the other, appeared to be paying them not the slightest attention. Her thoughts were in Andarahy: she already saw in imagination the wedding ceremony, the carriages, the elegantly turned out bridegroom, her own graceful charm, the inevitable wreath of orange blossoms in her hair; finally she was already adjusting her white dress and pinning on the veils of Malines lace that were to make both halves of the human species stare. She was awakened from this dream by her father's imprinting upon her forehead his second kiss. The first, as the reader will recall, was given her on the night after the counselor's death. The third would probably be bestowed on her wedding day.

"You know I love you, Eugenia?" said Camargo, gazing at her.

"Papa!"

He could not get out another word. His love, after one expansive moment, returned to its nest in the depth of his heart, where it had always been. His satisfaction required silence and seclusion in order to relish its own flavor. Now, Eugenia passed into Dona Thomazia's hands. Camargo's wife saw this marriage with far different eyes from those of her husband. What she saw in it, above all else, were the moral advantages to her daughter. She drew the girl down beside her and recited a catechism of duties and manners which Eugenia interrupted from time to time with excla-

mations of filial obedience: "Yes, mama! . . . Just you wait
. . . You'll see, mama! . . ."

Dona Thomazia savored her good luck. Her face, whose
expression was in general of a common, ordinary sort, on
this occasion had a something that turned it sublime. She
made her daughter sit on her lap, but Eugenia, feeling she
was too heavy a burden, slipped gently to the floor between
her mother's knees and remained looking up at her.

Camargo meanwhile was already no longer of this
world. He paced back and forth, his hands clasped behind
him, and kept biting the tips of his moustache. From time
to time, he glanced at the tableau formed by the two
ladies, but only mechanically; his dull gaze indicated he
was sunk in profound cogitation.

There was in that cynical, restrained, taciturn man a
true passion that was exclusive and ardent: it was his
daughter. Camargo adored Eugenia; she was his religion.
He had concentrated all his strength and all his thought on
making her happy. To achieve that end, he would not have
hesitated to employ, if necessary, violence, perfidy, and
deceit. Neither before nor since had he ever had a feeling
to equal it. He was never in love with his wife; he married
because matrimony is a serious and dignified condition.
The greatest friend he ever had was Counselor Valle; but
even the friendship that bound him to Estacio's father had
never received the acid test of sacrifice, yet, for all we
know, it might have been present in his character. He
knew only the, so to speak, stolid, homespun affections
such as neither know how nor have the strength to brave
life's stormy weather. In his spiritual relationships with
other human beings he possessed only the small change of
polite courtesies; the gold coin of great passions had never
found a place in his heart's strongbox—except for one, his
love of Eugenia.

But his love for his daughter, though violent, slavish,
and blind, was a way this father had of loving himself.

There entered into that love a large amount of fatuous vanity. Had she been less charming, Eugenia would perhaps have been less loved. He contemplated her with the same pride a goldsmith feels when he admires the jewel in its setting as it goes from beneath his hands. It was an egoist's tenderness: he loved himself in his own handiwork. Capricious, obstinate, and superficial, Eugenia never had the good fortune of seeing her defects corrected; rather, it was her upbringing that gave them to her. From Camargo's lips there never issued a word of correction; none of his actions revealed the vigilant, constant guidance that is the rightful prerogative of fatherhood. If his daughter's natural disposition had been bad her father's complicity would have made her worse.

It was not bad, luckily; her heart knew the sweet delights of kindness; her obstinacy was a habit, not an inborn fault. Even her frivolity had been developed by her upbringing, a mother's zealousness having little effect against the father's indulgences. It also explained the fascination exerted upon her by the giddy whirl of the temporal life. It might almost be said that she had never known short dresses; she was weaned by the modiste; a square dance was her first communion.

It was not an easy thing to give Eugenia the happiness that her father's ambition sought for her. Although he was not unthrifty, he could not scrape up enough to satisfy all his daughter's whims. For a long time he had been on the lookout for a husband, arming, at some expense, the cage into which the bird was to fall. The moment he perceived Estacio's inclination, he did all he could to catch and hold him. He waited many months for an initial move on Estacio's part and when that hope began to fly away into the region of problematical things he suspected Helena's influence. The girl had already greatly diminished his future son-in-law's inheritance; to wrest the son-in-law from him was too much. Camargo did not hesitate an instant; he made a direct attack. The result confirmed his suspicions.

The marriage was a great deal but it was not enough. Camargo had assumed a concern for Estacio's political career as a means of giving a certain enhancement to his daughter's importance and a retroactive consequence to himself, whose life had been more or less obscure. If Eugenia's husband were to confine himself to domestic repose between kitchen garden and algebra, Camargo's ambition would suffer immensely. We have seen him offer Estacio the political apple, which was refused at first; offered a second time it was finally accepted along with the bride. This double victory was the supreme moment of the doctor's life. He already heard the public applause, felt himself multiplied in size and importance; savored beforehand the sweets of notoriety, and saw himself, as it were, the father-in-law of his country and the father of its institutions.

"I am going to enter the lion's den but without Daniel's faith," sighed Estacio when he finally yielded to Camargo's persistent entreaties.

"Your talent will tame the lion."

It was agreed soon after that the wedding would take place in the first week of March. The two intervening months were allotted to ecclesiastical formalities and preparing the trousseau. Estacio accepted it all without objection. Dona Ursula and Helena approved the plan, but the aunt added a stipulation: the married couple were to come live with them in Andarahy.

Father Melchior, when consulted about the marriage, gave his full approval; only the interval of waiting seemed too long to him. The effusiveness with which he embraced Estacio and his words of praise made a lively impression on the young man. "You wanted this marriage very much?" he asked.

"Very much! Your father must approve it in heaven!"

Even the dead were conspiring against him. Estacio

resolutely accepted his fate. The priest's joy, usually moderate and dignified, went so far beyond its customary bounds as to appear almost childish. Dona Ursula was beside herself with satisfaction. Helena seemed to achieve her own happiness in this marriage. It was a universal bliss that Estacio was about to purchase at the price of everlasting chains.

Meanwhile, a temporary obstacle arose, the illness of Eugenia's godmother, the owner of a plantation in Cantagallo. It was she who had sent the above mentioned opal that one day shared the love and attention which the young lady should have devoted wholly to her future husband. The godmother was gravely ill, though less from the particular complaint at this time than from the years that weighed heavily upon her shoulders. She was a rich widow flanked by two unmarried nieces, a sister-in-law, a male cousin, the two sons of these last, and a score of goddaughters. From this, one may easily infer the slimness of Camargo's hopes. Although he had never neglected the duties imposed upon him by this spiritual bond, giving all possible proofs of a great affection; even so, it was to be feared that the dying woman's last wish might not bear the stamp of strict justice, or at least of reasonable fairness. Under these circumstances the trip to Cantagallo was most urgent, and it was incumbent upon him to make it no matter what the inconvenience. All inconveniences are pleasant when they terminate in a legacy. Camargo had not lost hope of such an outcome, at once friendly and pecuniary. He resolved to go to Cantagallo with his whole family, and advised his future son-in-law of it by letter.

Estacio welcomed the obstacle, but he did not count on what it bore in its belly. Arriving at Rio Comprido, he found the doctor and Dona Thomazia in great distress; Eugenia refused to leave the city. It was in vain that they pointed out to her the propriety of reciprocating her godmother's affection on this grave occasion; in vain they told her it would be ungrateful not to go receive the last breath of the venerable lady, her spiritual mother. Eugenia still flatly refused.

Her fiancé arrived during the final act of the struggle between parents and daughter. Eugenia's eyes were red with crying, she kept wringing her hands and declaring she would go only by force. Estacio tried to recall her to reason, seconding her father's arguments, without achieving more than he. Finally Eugenia placed a condition on her acquiescence: "I'll go if Dr. Estacio goes with us."

Camargo approved the condition *in petto;* verbally he opposed the sacrifice. Estacio, caught between the devil and the deep, now found Eugenia's trip superfluous.

"Come with us!" she insisted.

"Impossible!" interjected the doctor, "such an inconvenience to satisfy a mere whim!"

"Then I won't go!"

Dona Thomazia was annoyed, and ashamed of her daughter's obstinacy. Estacio bit his lip and glanced at the girl, whose eyes insistently questioned him. Decorum won out; looking upon Eugenia as his wife, he decided to cut short a scene that appeared ridiculous to him. "I'll go with you," he said without enthusiasm. The solution seemed a fair one; three of them cheerfully accepted it. The departure was set for two days from then. Dona Ursula, in spite of the favor with which she regarded the marriage, found her nephew's departure unnecessary but she did not attempt to dissuade him. Helena approved of the whole thing. The bridegroom made his two relatives sensible of the extent of his sacrifice and was even on the point of withdrawing his promise. It was too late. The last night he passed in Andarahy was cruel for him; the hours flew by more quickly than ever before. As he had to leave early the next morning, he said goodbye to his aunt and sister that night, a goodbye for a few days that was as painful to him as if it had been for years. He promised, however, that he would return shortly.

But it was not possible for him to promise to conjure away the drama that was preparing in the wings — a drama that would unfold in intense, sinister, inevitable catastrophe, with no consolation for him ever — either in the sweet rewards of domestic peace or in the glories of public life.

## Chapter XV

He got up at dawn. Once ready, he decided to surprise his aunt and his sister with a last remembrance, and wrote these words on a piece of paper, "Goodbye till I return, 6 o'clock in the morning." He folded it and went and placed it on the table in Dona Ursula's sewing room. From there he passed into the dining room and out on the veranda, where he caught sight of Helena waiting for him at the head of the veranda stairs.

"Sh!" she said softly. "Don't be surprised and make a noise that might wake aunty. I came to see if you needed anything."

"Nothing," he answered, deeply touched. "But what foolishness is this to get up so early?"

"Early! The sun is almost up. Goodbye! Many remembrances to Eugenia. You don't need anything?"

"Nothing." He took the hand she held out to him and stood looking at her.

"Look, it is late!" As she spoke she pressed his hand and sought to withdraw her own; Estacio retained it.

"If you knew how hard it is for me to go!"

"It's only for a few days . . ."

"It will seem like months, Helena! Goodbye, don't forget

me. Write me. I will write as soon as I arrive. Don't do anything foolhardy; don't go out riding while I am away."

"Goodbye!"

"Goodbye!" Estacio started to give her a farewell hug but
she stopped him, less by word than by gesture.

"No," said she drawing back, "long farewells are the
hardest to endure." She moved away, as far as the door to
the dining room, waved goodbye and went inside. Estacio
slowly descended the stairs. Helena watched him go down
and saw him leave. Then she cautiously tiptoed upstairs to
her own quarters. There she sat some minutes, pensive and
sad. Finally she got up, quickly put on her riding habit, set
the little black hat on her loosely combed hair, and went
down to the chácara. Vicente was waiting for her with the
mare already saddled. Helena mounted without delay, the
page leapt up on his mule, and the two riders went off at a
trot in the direction of the cottage with the old-fashioned
penthouse and blue flag.

There, all was still. The windows were hermetically
sealed. Helena dismounted and gently knocked, then repeated the blows, which became progressively louder. No
one answered. She hastily went around the house, but it
would seem she found the doors at the rear also closed, for
she came right back. She put her ear to the door and
waited. When it became apparent that all her efforts were
in vain, she took a pencil and a little piece of paper out of
her pocket, set her foot on the tiled step, and with the
paper on her knee wrote a few words, doubled the paper
and slipped it under the door. She waited a few minutes
longer, then walked over to the mare, mounted and returned home.

Her ride was sad and thoughtful. The mare, jogging at a
languid pace, did not feel the rider's usual vigor, her reins
slack, the whip idle. The page kept his eyes on his mistress
with a look of visible adoration; but, at the same time, with
the license conferred by confidence and complicity he

puffed on a big Havana cigar extracted from the master's humidor.

Dona Ursula was not yet up. Helena did not conceal the morning's ride from her. The day dragged on sad and lonely, like those that followed, in spite of the thoughtfulness of family friends who came to keep the two ladies company. Mendonça, to whose special care Estacio had recommended them, was punctual in the discharge of that obligation. He managed to assuage somewhat their longing for the absent one. Father Melchior lengthened his daily visits.

All shared the same feeling, but it was not the only feeling to be found among them. A sentiment of a different sort, private and egoistic, had taken root in one of them. Mendonça felt that half of his destiny had ended, that the second half was about to begin and that it would be more prudent and discreet than the first half. The clock on which he saw the fateful hour about to strike was Helena's eyes. Mendonça was falling in love. Reckless and irresponsible but not dissolute, he had passed through his early years without losing the flower of pure love, without even having plucked it. Helena sensed the birth of his silent adoration and saw it grow, but pretended not to see. She did not encourage him, she did not repulse him; she redoubled their intimacy—the intimacy one grants to old, trusted friends, but plainly shows a man in love the emptiness of his hopes. To others' eyes, there was perfect accord between them. The colonel major winked one eye at Dr. Mattos; Dr. Mattos muttered a *latet anguis in herba,* and they went together to share the bread of their reflections with the lawyer's wife, a lady very sagacious in parlor romances. Their unanimous opinion was that the marriage was probable, and perhaps certain. There could be only one obstacle, that is, objections on the part of Mendonça's father. That obstacle, however, did not exist; besides the young lady's estimable qualities, there was the recognition, legal and social, public and private; in addition to which (an observation of Dr. Mattos') two hundred-plus gilt-edged securities deserve a tipping of the hat and do not require five minutes' reflection.

The first letters from Estacio arrived one afternoon when the two ladies and Mendonça sat on the veranda after dinner, drinking their last drops of coffee. Dona Ursula, after bustling off three mucamas to go look for her glasses, got up and went to look for them herself with her letter in her hand. Helena, still seated near one of the windows, opened hers and read it to herself:

"When this letter reaches your hands I shall be dying of longing for my aunt and for you. My own people, my house, my books, my cherished daily habits—these are my life. I never felt it so much as now that I am far from what is dearest to me in this world. A few days have gone by and it already seems like months. What would the separation be if it were not to be so short?

"In the letter I am writing aunty I give an account of our trip and of everyone's health. Dona Clara is indeed near death but she may still live some days, and Dr. Camargo is determined to wait until we can bid her a final farewell. Her family has given us a most cordial welcome. There are presently here her sister-in-law, a cousin, three nephews, other relatives, and various godsons and goddaughters. The cousin is a decorated lieutenant colonel; he and the others are the most affable people in the world. The men of this family have political influence. When they learned of my candidacy, they immediately offered their services, with the single stipulation of there being a previous recommendation from Rio de Janeiro. I thanked them from the bottom of my heart because in the case of a candidacy which never had any attraction for me, and still does not, there is no remedy except to give it my best efforts, lest my name suffer the ignominy of defeat. How do you like that for a touch of vanity?

"Let us change the subject, as it is one that distresses me

and I do not wish to debate the matter without you who are my companion in these mental wanderings. There, far from me, you perhaps do not remember our conversations; here everything is remembered. Each morning I have my ride on horseback, as I did there, but what a difference! The person riding at my side is the lieutenant colonel, an excellent good-hearted fellow with the single defect, and it is an enormous one, that his name is not Dona Helena do Valle, that he is not my darling Helena; she is back there in the city, enjoying herself without her brother. The colonel talks about everything, and at length: coffee, the government, elections, slavery, taxes. I listen—which is the least I can do—and let him go on without interruption. Sometimes, as if distrustful and offended, he withdraws into silence; then I pick up the thread of his talk and tie it together, and he cheerfully goes on unrolling it from the spool. So little a thing makes him happy! I went hunting once; I'll admit, to you, that it is the one thing that can distract me. I thought I had lost the knack for it but I have not. Modesty prevents me from saying more.

"The plantation is vast in extent and the house excellent. I will not say that I enjoy country life; I don't. It is not to my taste. But, to live in a retired spot like this at two paces from the woods and as many leagues from the Rua do Ouvidor, that, I believe, would suit my humor. We must consult aunty. I do not know what it is to love the tumult of the outside world; I find it dissipates one's being and nips the budding flower of sentiment. I was born to be a monk . . . and also, I believe, a despot, because here I am planning an obscure, lonely life without consulting your preferences. I am a Cromwell with a friar's inclinations, or, to sum it up in a word, I am a Luther . . . on a much lower scale.

"Poor Helena! Already four whole pages, all about me! Let us see what you have been doing. Do you feel very sad? Do you go out much? Read? Play games? Play the piano?

Give me an account of your life in the most minute detail possible. Tell me about the others. Do not keep anything from me. If, for example, when you open a book or play a note on the piano you think of me, write me of it, marking the day and even the hour if you can. And now I give you leave to ask me where my gravity has gone. I will answer that there is a serious childishness, and that extremes meet. If this should not happen with me it is the fault of heaven, which did not give me a baby sister; now we must begin the first phase of life.

"I earnestly requested Mendonça to visit our house often. I do not know whether he has remembered and kept his promise to me. If he has not, you must send him word that I detest and abominate him, that he is the biggest traitor under the sun, that all is over between us, that friendship is a sacred cult to be tended with daily rites, etc. Tell him whatever you think best and in your own style.

"I am reminded of you by everything. This afternoon, for example, the landscape offered a beautiful characteristic view. If she were here, I said to myself, she would make a magnificent drawing. I took a pencil I had with me and a half-sheet of paper and decided to reproduce the panorama. What I put on the paper was an algebraic problem! That was the advice given me by the pencil; no one should set himself to do something he knows nothing about. I did not know what it was to be absent from my family. Why did I decide to try it?

"I just interrupted this letter to speak with Dr. Froes, Dona Clara's physician. He came to my room to tell me that his patient's condition is hopeless, that death is certain but that she may live many days. What a prospect! I am furious with myself; these final days of the sick woman's weigh upon me like fate's clenched fist. If death is certain why live a few days more? Is that life, or is it death a sip at a time, without knowledge of what you are losing or of what is in store for you?

"It's final: I may leave here in six days or in a month, as God wills. Meanwhile send me some books. The only thing I find in my room is a *Manual of Practical Medicine*. Send me something that will remind me of Andarahy. Take eight or ten volumes from the bookcase; choose for me. Send me, also, some of your needlework to show Dona Clara's sister-in-law. I have been bragging a lot to her about your accomplishments. If you could make a sketch of something in a hurry, the cistern, the veranda, or some other place, do so and send it along with the rest of the things. Write me at length; tell me anything that might be of interest. Tell me about yourself, that will be the best way to relieve my longing, which is immeasurable, immeasurable as this love I have for all my family. I am going to try my utmost to come back soon. Goodbye, my darling Helena, goodbye my life; goodbye most beautiful and gentle of all sisters!

"P.S. I have reread this letter and am ashamed of the part regarding the invalid's life. Forgive my ferocity and put it down to loneliness."

## Chapter XVI

Helena read and reread the letter. Then she sat silently gazing at the leaves of the vine which had climbed up the outside wall and curled over the sill into the veranda. The letter remained open on her knees. Mendonça, a few feet away, looked at her without venturing to speak to her.

Goethe once wrote that the vertical line is the law of human intelligence. One may say by the same token that the curved line is the law of feminine grace. Mendonça felt this to be so as he contemplated Helena's figure with its chaste undulating rhythm of shoulder and bosom beneath the fine muslin of her dress. She was leaning forward slightly. From his position Mendonça could see her correct, pensive profile, the soft curve of her arm, the indiscreetly inquisitive tip of her little satin slipper. The attitude suited her melancholy beauty. He gazed at her without moving, without speaking.

The afternoon was expiring, the green of the hill opposite had taken on the dark gray look that precedes the disappearance of all color into night's darkness. Night itself was at hand; a slave entered the veranda to light the two great lamps that hung from its ceiling. This circumstance aroused Helena enough to make her turn her head and see Estacio's friend a few feet away.

"You have been there all the time?" she asked nervously.

"Dona Ursula did not come back," he replied hesitantly. "I was unwilling to interrupt your reading."

"Reading? The reading ended a long time ago."

"But one also reads by heart."

Helena shot a suspicious glance at him. "I do not know how to read by heart," she said. She rose and left the veranda.

Mendonça was dumbfounded. What could he have said of such a serious nature as to offend her? He mentally went over the words he had spoken and found nothing wrong with them. Certain, however, that he *had* offended her, he stood there annoyed with himself, desirous of explaining it all to her, if there was anything explainable. After a few moments he decided to follow her into the house. He went in. Helena was not in the dining room, nor in the card room, where he found Dona Ursula with Dr. Mattos and the colonel major. He went on into the drawing room. Helena did not see him enter; she was sunk in a big easy chair with her head in her hands. Touched and shaken, he checked his step and contemplated her for several moments, then he walked toward her and spoke to her. Helena raised her head. "Forgive me," he said, "if I said something that offended you. I must confess, I do not know what it could have been. Were you disturbed by something I said?"

She fixed him with a look that was still full of suspicion and did not immediately reply. Mendonça adopted the best course in such a situation; he bowed and turned to leave. Helena called to him. He went up to her once more, with such a gentle air of resignation that it would have softened the most exalted pride. Helena held out her hand to him. He grasped it warmly and had an urge to kiss it, once and many times, triumphing in that one instant over his hesitation of many days, but his courage failed him. Helena showed him the part of Estacio's letter that referred to him. They spoke of their absent friends and of those present, of everyone and everything except the matter that exclusively absorbed the young man's thoughts. He left her without having said a word of what was in his heart. As he stepped into the street, he suddenly felt how craven and ridiculous he had been and he called himself a thousand bad names. Finally he promised to lay his whole soul before her the next day.

The next day, it was a Sunday, Helena went to the chapel to hear Mass by Father Melchior. After the ceremony she did not go home with Dona Ursula but went into the sacristy, where the priest had been removing his vestments. As soon as he learned of Estacio's letter, he asked Helena to let him see it. "Friends' letters always speak directly to the heart," he explained.

Helena gave him the letter, which he received with a look more of curiosity than friendly interest. He read it slowly as if scrutinizing every word for its meaning, and since it was a long letter the time he spent interpreting was also long. Meanwhile, Helena sat admiring his austere figure, his religious serenity. The sacristy was small; two high windows let in light and air and the aroma of the foliage and flowers out on the chácara. Between the entablature and the tiled roof some swallows had built their nest and now came forth like youthful thoughts to flutter in the morning sun. Beside that external scene of joy and verdure the sacristy had a certain air of severe melancholy that cast over one's soul a forgetfulness of human vicissitudes. Helena let herself be captivated by that feeling of exalted abstention; if some grief or remorse tormented her she forgot it, for a minute at least, between those plain unadorned walls, in the presence of a priest—between an image of Jesus and the Creator's living works.

When he had read the letter, Melchior folded it up with a thoughtful air and handed it back to her. "Have you written an answer?" he asked.

"Yes. I have brought you the letter I am going to send off this very day."

Melchior opened it and read, spending no less time than on the other, although it was much shorter. The style was affectionate but much less effusive than that of Estacio's letter. She related, in its general aspects, the life they had led since he left, their daily occupations and their pastimes in the evening. "We live (she wrote) as two people can who know the love a dear relative has for them though absent, absent but not forgotten nor forgetting. Father Melchior, one or other neighbor, and Dr. Mendonça are our habitual visitors. You know what our priest is—the most beautiful soul God ever sent to the world. The neighbors are affable as always. Dr. Mendonça is truly worthy of our affection and trust. I told him what you wrote; he laughed like a man sure of escaping punishment.

"It is a pity you have to stay such a long time but if there is some hope of saving the sick woman, we shall consider ourselves well repaid for the long delay. It is true you are not a physician but there is another sick lady there for whom you *are* not only physician but also the whole pharmacopoeia. Why hasn't Eugenia written me? I did not think this friend of mine would forget me on the eve of becoming my sister-in-law. If she were not so far away I would go pull her ears. Tell her I said so. And if you have an opportunity to lend me your fingers, punish her for me, stating her crime and the judge who sentenced her.

"What you say about the life of solitude is very true but impracticable. Our friends would not come to see us, and could we do without them? That is aunty's opinion as well as mine. The best thing of all is this middle term of Andarahy: we are neither out of the world nor in the midst of it. The noisy bustle outside may have the effect you speak of but at times it is necessary to deafen and distract the spirit. Solitude too has its aches and pains; it too troubles the heart. Neither one extreme nor the other."

The letter contained a few sentences more, not many. Three or four times she spoke of Eugenia, with such insistence that it placed in relief Estacio's silence on the subject; she spoke to him of his bride's beauty, of their approaching marriage, of the love that would make their happiness and the joyful satisfaction it would give those most near to them.

When the priest finished reading Helena's answer he opened his arms to her. Then he took her face in his hands and contemplated her for several moments. "Your whole soul is in that letter," said he. "I see in it thoughtfulness and love. Very good! There is, however, one thing missing; you did not send your brother remembrances from me. There is also one thing too much; you praise merits that I do not possess. Never mind! Send it . . ."

"I'll add a couple of lines."

"Yes, and tell him to hurry up, because I am old and may die before . . ."

"Oh!" protested Helena.

Melchior gazed at her in silence. "Do you think Estacio will be happy?" he finally asked.

"I do."

"I too."

Another silence. Broken at last by the priest. "Why don't you marry also?" said he.

"I?"

"Yes, you. Perhaps, in a short while . . ."

"Perhaps never."

Melchior frowned. His countenance, ordinarily kind and gentle, became stern as his conscience. He was holding one of Helena's hands in his; he unconsciously let it drop. And there rose between them a silence that oppressed them and that neither dared break; as if overpowered by a mystery, each feared what the other might read in his face, and they instinctively averted their eyes.

Melchior was the first to return to himself. Reflection corrected impulse, and the priest again assumed his usual mien with that dissimulation which is a duty when sincerity is dangerous. "Well, who knows?" he said. "No one can decide what he will do tomorrow. God writes the pages of our destiny; we do no more than copy them out on earth."

"That's true!" she agreed with a movement of her head, but without raising her eyes.

"Tomorrow," the priest continued, "chance—what the nonbelievers call chance is actually the considered decision of the Infinite Will—may show you a man worthy of you, and your heart will say to you, 'This is he,' and your dispirited sigh of today will turn into a grateful glance toward heaven. Well, all I ask, all I wish is that he hurry up and come in time for me to marry you . . ."

"Oh! But you are not going to die tomorrow," interrupted Helena.

"I am old, my child. These white hairs are the snowy mist of that polar sea we all must navigate. I am sixty years old. Death may gather me in any day now . . ."

"It's time for breakfast," said Helena with a smile.

They left the sacristy, went through the chapel and out into the chácara. As they were about to cross the chapel threshold, they saw Mendonça enter the Valle house. Melchior checked his step and glanced at Helena. She appeared depressed and deep in thought. The priest's expression when she told him that she would perhaps never marry remained engraved on her memory like an enigma that she feared to decipher. Only a few minutes had passed; nevertheless she had been able to reflect and arrive at a decision. Stopping beside the priest in the chapel doorway, she too saw Mendonça enter the house. Once again her eyes questioned those of the priest and his questioned hers, but this time neither averted their glance.

"Do you see that man?" she asked. "Do you think he would make a good husband?"

"Excellent, no doubt," Melchior quickly answered, "his character, upbringing, attitudes . . ."

"He has still another, special, virtue: he is in love with me."

"I know."

"He told you?"

"No, but it is apparent. It is known to everyone who frequents this house. The probability of the marriage is a subject of remark; the general opinion is that it will take place in a short time. Has he made some sort of declaration to you?"

"No, nothing of the sort, but a woman's eyes, when she is the object of a man's love, are no less sagacious than those of friendly priests. Do you think I ought to confirm our friends' opinions?"

"Yes, I do. You should, however, consult your own heart."

"I have done so."

"In this one instant?"

"That's right."

"Truly?" he asked, and he gazed at Helena's serious countenance with a look of fatherly tenderness.

"I do not say that I am in love with him at the moment, but his love for me will find an echo in my heart and I shall come to love him. What is important to know is that he is worthy of me. Of all those who aspire to my hand, none is his superior."

"Very well! And yet, bear in mind that you are going to contract a perpetual obligation and that a contract of this kind cannot be decided upon in a few seconds."

"Oh! on that point my ignorance is more learned than your theology. What are minutes? what are months? Passions of many years, arriving at matrimony, often end in separation or hatred, or at best in indifference. Love is no more than a means of choice, to love is to choose a fellow-being to be a companion throughout life, not to assure the everlasting happiness of two persons, because that may vanish or change. What remains in most marriages after the first years of passion? A calm affection, esteem, the closeness of familiarity. I ask no more of marriage, nor can I give more than this."

"I do not like to see so much reflectiveness in such green years," Melchior replied benevolently, "and yet your reasoning enchants me, and when all is said and done may be correct. But I do not retract what I said: a few minutes is too little time; reflect at least for twenty-four hours."

"No, not an instant more," insisted Helena. "My reflections are either slow or sudden, either five minutes or a year. Take your choice."

"Well then, reflect for five minutes," he smilingly replied.

"Four of them have already gone by! I shall seize the last one to tell you that I would have said none of this if it were not for the young man's outstanding qualities, and I will add that a certain sympathy in our natures attracts me to him . . . perhaps it is the seed of love."

They had arrived at the foot of the veranda stairs. They went up and entered the dining room, where they found Dona Ursula and Mendonça, the latter running his eyes over the morning paper. Breakfast was served immediately.

"Reverend Father," said Dona Ursula, "you two delayed so long that I thought . . . you had got some idea of stealing Helena from me."

"I was hearing her confession," Melchior answered.

"And you found it possible to absolve her?"

"Of course."

"But with a big penance, huh?"

"The easiest there is," interjected Helena, looking at the priest.

"Oh! then it must be her sins are trifling ones," concluded Dona Ursula. "Don't you think so?" This last was directed to Mendonça, as they all approached the table. Mendonça made no answer. Contrary to his usual custom he spoke little, even less than on the day before and on the days before that. Dona Ursula noticed the difference but could not explain it. "I don't want to know what sins she confessed to," she said, seating herself at the table. "I am sure the worst of them would not put anyone in Purgatory."

"Just see what an indulgent aunt is," observed Helena to Mendonça, taking the place next to him.

Preoccupied with the conversation he had had in the sacristy and as they came across the chácara, Melchior at first paid little attention to the merchant's son. He was busy analyzing the circumstances of the moment and weighing the responsibility that might devolve upon him of coming to some kind of decision. After a long dialogue with his conscience, the old priest bent his gaze on the young lover, who sat opposite, next to Helena. He saw them converse. She appeared gracious, solicitous, and attentive, like a loving wife. He appeared enamoured of her voice and style of speaking, as if a sudden clear light within had revealed to his soul the infinite horizons of hope. Accepted on familiar terms by Helena and treated with exquisite attention by her . . . it was, after all, the first time she had spoken to him, not as to a trusted friend but as to a man who might come to be her husband. A certain seriousness, a submissive glance, a constant attentiveness, were what made the difference which was felt by the heart rather than seen with the eyes.

After breakfast Melchior went into the drawing room with Helena. Mendonça accompanied them. The priest's resolve was firmly rooted; he accepted this marriage as a gift from heaven. They were scarcely inside the room when he grasped their hands and said to them in a tone of deep emotion, "Will you promise not to be angry with me?"

Mendonça's eyes asked, "For what?" Helena lowered *hers*.

"Do you promise?"

"Reverend Father . . ." Mendonça began, and could not finish the sentence.

The priest glanced silently at one and then the other. Perhaps he was hesitant about speaking; perhaps he was searching for the best way of saying what he had in his heart. It was urgent to break the silence; he did it with solemnity:

"Doubtless I am twice ordained a priest, by nature and by the Gospel. When two beings are worthy of each other it is a service to God to lend a voice to the heart that does not dare speak. You, sir, love this girl; I can read in your eyes the feeling that draws you to her. You and she deserve to be happy together. If it is reticence that closes your lips, my son, I am the voice of truth and infinite love. If some other motive holds you silent, I shall be a complaisant judge to hear it."

Mendonça was thunderstruck by the priest's words, and remained mute. Not only did good fortune come to him when he least expected it but she had even chosen a strange, unused path. Reality was becoming confused with dream. The presence of a third person was sufficient reason to overwhelm the most resolute man; add the sacred, priestly dress, which gave the scene an air of solemn consecration. Mendonça finally recovered the use of his senses, and his response was eloquent: he held out his hand to Helena. She returned his gesture with a like one that was simple and natural.

"My eyes did not deceive me," said the priest. "You love this girl and can give her the happiness that I desire for her. And she will make your happiness. Won't you?" he asked, turning to Helena.

Mendonça had finally found his voice. "Is this a dream?" he said.

"Life is nothing else," retorted Melchior. "An old thought, an old truth. Let us see to it that the dream be pleasant, not arid or sad. Do you both promise me to make each other happy?"

"It will be my sole ambition," returned the young man, "my whole concern and my glory."

"Your love," Melchior went on, "is stronger than Helena's. I have consulted her and read her heart. She chooses you with contentment and satisfaction but without rapture. It is not blind passion that caused her to speak; it is a tender, sincere sentiment and for that very reason will endure. The reflectiveness of the one will counteract the other's impetuousness, and the two emotions will complete one another, each with its own special virtue."

This frank explanation of Melchior's had the charm of being agreeable to both. Helena rejoiced that he had neither flattered Mendonça's illusions nor represented her as accepting the proposed marriage with unreflecting indifference. Mendonça, for his part, saw in the priest's words proof of Helena's sincerity and accepted the little offered him with a certainty of making it increase. Melchior's character and the veneration owed his virtuous life were warranty of his truthfulness and gave their simple transaction a strong stamp of sanctity and high-mindedness. It was not an ordinary declaration of love, subject to variations of emotion or of interest; it was a true betrothal with religion its inspiration and witness.

## *Chapter XVII*

That day was marked on Mendonça's calendar in letters of gold and vermillion; night came crowned with myrtle and roses. He lived the whole time in a state of somnambulism and ecstasy. He had intended to tell it all to his mother as soon as he entered the house at midday but was afraid to because he was not actually sure if it was a living reality or if he was flying on the wings of a chimera. That night, he went back to Andarahy. He found in Helena the same affectionate manner, the same solicitude and loving attentions, not an expansive tenderness, not the contemplative look of a woman in love—a middle term that held him within bounds but nonetheless touched his heart. The new situation was, meanwhile, perceptible to others. The watchful ones exchanged glances full of grave discoveries. One among them, the colonel major, even gave voice to a broad hint which the interested parties pretended not to understand.

Mendonça went home that night still more excited than before, his senses swimming in a bath of glory. The city, as he entered it, seemed transformed by a magic wand. He saw it peopled with fantastic, shimmering beings who went back and forth from heaven to earth and from earth to heaven. The color of the sky was unique among all the hues on the divine scene-painter's palette. The stars seemed to greet him with great fans of electricity, or to taunt him with vulgar gestures, out of envy and spite. Invisible wings brushed his hair. Voices without mouths spoke to his heart. His feet seemed scarcely to touch the ground; he wandered in ecstasy beyond his knowledge. Was this the jolly vagabond of a short time ago? Love had performed one more of its miracles.

A theater was open. He bought a ticket and went in, not that he wanted to be amused or to lose himself in the play, which, what is more, was on the point of expiring in a mutual homicide pact with the protagonist. It was a need to see people, to run his hands over reality, so chimerical did all that had passed since morning appear to him.

A fellow spectator, the colonel major's son, saw him from a distance and came and sat down beside him. "You, sir, who have better eyesight," said the student, "tell me if I'm wrong; isn't that young lady over there in the box the passenger-pigeon?"

"Passenger-pigeon?" Mendonça repeated, staring at him. "What does that mean?"

"It's the nickname for Estacio's sister. Would that be she sitting over there with an elderly lady?"

"But why do they call her by such a name?"

"How should I know? Probably because she goes out riding every day. Quite a ride when you come to think of it! At the break of dawn, and there she goes on her little horse with the page following . . ."

"Who gave her that nickname?"

"Nicknames are like anonymous newspaper attacks; they have no author."

When the curtain fell Mendonça took leave of him at once and went out of the theater. In the street, he mentally repeated what the boy had said. After a few minutes, he smiled; he understood that though a mere suspicion of his happiness had got abroad, envy had already put a drop of poison in the cup. He shrugged and calmly accepted success's livid companion.

He started for home and arrived soon after. Helena had again taken complete possession of his thought. Alone, in his bachelor's bedroom, he went over the events of the day and decided he was fortune's favorite son. As he had to talk to someone, he wrote a long letter to Estacio, relating the whole story of his heart, his hopes and their prompt realization. His whole soul spilled out on the paper, impetuous and exuberant. The style was uneven, the usage faulty but it had the eloquence and sincerity of passion. As he sealed the letter he saw in advance the pleasure it would give his friend when it came to his hand, bringing word that the tie formed between them in the classroom would become stronger and still more close in the family. "Come as soon as you can," he wrote in closing, "I am anxious to embrace you and hear from your own lips the consent that will make me the happiest of men!"

When the letter reached Cantagallo, Estacio had just returned from a little side trip with Eugenia's father. He recognized the handwriting of the superscription and negligently opened the letter. He read it with dismay. The impression made on him was so visible that Camargo asked him what was the matter.

"I have received a piece of news that obliges me to leave tomorrow," he replied.

"A serious matter?"

"Yes."

"Even so, at a time like this . . ."

"Where's the harm? Dona Clara may hold off death for some days yet. And, although my absence does not affect the matter to which I have reference, still it is imperative for me to inform myself and take proper steps."

"Some business relative to the inventory," ventured Camargo, who knew of nothing more serious than money.

"Just so," Estacio answered mechanically.

Camargo consoled his daughter for the disappointment caused by her fiancé's departure; he spoke the language of reason; he said there were practical business matters to which the sentiments of the heart had to give way sometimes. The following morning Estacio left for the city, but not without promising to return if Dona Clara's illness or any other motive obliged the family to remain in Cantagallo.

No one expected him in Andarahy. On entering the grounds (it was night) Estacio saw that the drawing room, which was located in the left-hand corner at the front of the house, was lighted up and there were people in it. This room was on the ground floor and the windows were open. He stopped a few feet away and could make out the colonel major and Dr. Mattos playing backgammon, the lawyer's wife talking to Dona Ursula and Melchior on one side of the room; on the other sat Helena with Mendonça facing her.

Estacio went around to the rear of the house and entered by the veranda. The slaves who saw him come signaled his presence with their cries of joy. The sound, however, did not reach the people in the drawing room. They knew nothing of his arrival until he appeared in the doorway of the room. The pleasure at seeing him was general, and sincere on the part of everyone. Estacio distributed hugs and handshakes. Melchior, who remained standing to one side, was the last person with whom he spoke.

"Did Dr. Camargo come back?" Dona Ursula asked her nephew as soon as he had paid his respects to everyone.

"No," Estacio answered. "There is no hope for the sick lady's recovery, but she was still alive when I left."

"I can imagine the heirs' impatience!"

This philosophic observation by the colonel major passed without notice. Melchior, who inwardly disapproved of it, changed the subject, asking after the Camargo family. Estacio gave all the news that might be of interest, then spoke of things that happened on the trip back, and finally withdrew to his room for a few minutes.

Mendonça followed his friend, overtaking him on the stairs. They went up together and together entered the bedroom.

"Now that we are alone," said Mendonça, "did something happen there?"

"No, nothing."

"That's good!"

A slave entered the room to help his master dress. Men-

donça, though anxious to speak of Helena, contented himself with throwing out a few vague remarks.

"Did you receive my letter?" he asked.

"Yes."

"You weren't expecting it, I'll wager..."

"No."

"Just as I didn't expect to write it. Are you annoyed
about something?"

"I'm tired."

"Of course," assented Mendonça, opening a book that
was lying on the table and closing it again.

The silence lengthened into minutes: Mendonça again
opened the book, examined a hunting rifle, rolled a ciga-
rette and lighted it. The slave went on helping his master
change. Estacio continued deadly silent. Mendonça spoke
once or twice about indifferent matters, but the time did
not hurry past, it traveled with the lagging step it usually
does when it has to do with impatient men. As soon as
Estacio was dressed and the slave went out of the room,
Mendonça turned directly to the matter that preoccupied
him. "I was anxious to see you," said he. "It is not possible
to talk now; we do not have time, but I want to give you a
hug at least, a hug of thanks for the happiness..."

"It seems that you were only waiting for my absence,
eh?"

"No, I don't think so. Even before you left, I was beginning to have a new feeling that I came to see was a violent
love."

"Does Helena love you?"

"With an equal love, no, I don't think so; but she
accepts me, she has an affection for me."

"I'll consult her about it myself."

Mendonça was prevented from speaking further because
Estacio was already descending the stairs when he threw
out that last remark. Mendonça went down also. The same
persons were gathered in the drawing room. Helena stood

near a window conversing with the priest. Tea was served and the conversation became general, though not at all animated. Melchior spoke less than the others. Even so, he was not the first to leave, he was the last. As he walked toward the chácara gate, he raised his eyes to the firmament, not to see the moon and the stars, but to go beyond to the region above. What he said, no one knew, but the angel in charge of human petitions perchance gathered the venerable old priest's thoughts into his bosom and carried them to lay at the feet of Eternal Chaste Love.

## Chapter XVIII

"Helena," said Estacio the next day as soon as he found his sister alone, "do you know why I came back so suddenly? It was because of you. Mendonça wrote me that he had won a promise of marriage from you."

"It's true."

"It's true?"

"To the limit of my will, that is, your will. I can decide nothing by myself alone; but I do not believe you will offer any opposition. Surely you wish me to be happy?"

They were sitting on a wooden bench beside the huge cistern. For some time Estacio remained staring at the water. "I don't understand," he said finally.

"What?"

"More than once I have heard you confess to a violent passion, a love that seemed to possess your whole being. Although it is unusual for a woman, in spite of a single, strong love, to marry a man who is not the first of her heart, many times it is justifiable. But that such a marriage make her happiness—this I confess I shall never be able to understand."

"Then you refuse your consent?"

"No, I only want to understand."

"Nothing more simple," she replied.

"Ah!"

"I spoke to you of a strong love, it is true, not extinct at that time but totally without hope. What girl does not have these fancies, at least once? The fancy passed. Either I am never to marry or I can marry a worthy man who loves me. For a time it was my wish not to marry. This is no longer so since you, aunty, and Father Melchior all want to see me married and happy. To obtain happiness with marriage, I chose a person who seems to me capable of bringing peace to our home along with the best of his heart's affection."

"That is, you sacrifice yourself to our wishes?"

"Even if it were a sacrifice I would do it, gladly; but it is not."

"It is not a question of a repugnant and hateful sacrifice, still one must consider what you lose. You say your fancy has passed. I don't believe it, Helena, I don't believe it is dead. You are still in love, violently in love with someone, but it is a love without hope, without future; that is, you will bring to your husband's house a heart that does not belong to you, and a feeling that is intrusive and unfriendly..."

Helena tried to interrupt him. "Listen," he continued, "if it happens that this feeling dies and is replaced by a growing affection for your husband, you will not be unhappy; but suppose the old love does not die, what will your situation be then?"

"All this is a castle in the air," said Helena smiling. "I *was* in love, I am not in love, or, I love only my future husband."

Estacio shook his head with an air of disbelief. His eyes fastened upon his sister's placid features as if trying to wrest from them a mute confession. Her eyes, firm and tranquil, met his in a steady gaze. Estacio was already familiar with the control this young girl exercised over herself; her tranquility did not convince him. He told her so without mincing words.

"Why would I deny the truth?" retorted Helena.

Estacio shrugged his shoulders.

"Supposing you are right," she continued, "am I never to marry?"

"I don't say that, but there are two other paths to happiness besides Mendonça."

"I don't see them."

"Are you sure this mysterious love is really without hope? Nothing in the world is absolutely fixed and unchangeable —neither misfortune nor prosperity. What you imagine lost may only be strayed or hidden from sight . . ."

"I can guess what your second path is," interposed Helena; "by not marrying now I may one day come to love, more than Mendonça, some man as worthy as he."

"Does that seem absurd to you?"

"No, but it is a gamble: I exchange a certain good for a doubtful one, it is the reasoning of a gamester. That happiness of yours may never come; I am content with the happiness offered me now. Mendonça truly loves me; I have been aware of it for some time. Father Melchior opened my eyes. I accept the destiny these two propose for me. This is reason and reality; the rest is illusion and fantasy."

While she spoke Estacio had taken off his Panama hat and kept circulating its band round and round the crown. There was deep silence between them. On the edge of the cistern marched a long column of ants, most of them carrying pieces of green leaves. With a dry twig Estacio absently broke up the poor animals' silent, laborious march. They fled, some to the land side, some toward the water, while the rest hastened to press on in the direction of their domicile. Helena snatched the twig from his hand; Estacio appeared to rouse from a lengthy reflection; he stood up, took a few steps, and came back to her. "Helena," he declared, "I do not believe a word of what you just said; you are sacrificing yourself needlessly and ingloriously. I will not consent to it. It is my duty to oppose such a thing . . ."

Helena also rose. "Mendonça is beginning to be forbidden fruit," she observed, smiling. "It is the surest way to make one love him." She moved away, in the direction of the house. Estacio saw her disappear among the trees and remained a while longer, standing between the bench and the cistern. The ants, dispersed a few minutes before, had now returned to their former path and in the same precise formation. The young gentleman observed them and compared them to his own ideas which also required that an invisible twig should cease to scatter and confuse them. In the midst of his reflections, he bethought him of the priest. He crossed the chácara, came out on the street and started toward Melchior's house.

Melchior lived in a little cottage situated in the center of a diminutive garden, just a few yards from Estacio's residence. It had two rooms, windows on all sides, a door in front and a door at the back. The front door was located between two windows with Venetian blinds. The sitting room was also a study and workroom. The furniture was simple: no ornaments, a bookcase of jacarandá with huge quarto and folio volumes in it, a secretary, two easy chairs, and little else.

When Estacio entered he found Melchior walking back and forth with an open book in his hands, a Tertullian or Augustine or some other author of like stature, for the priest loved to contemplate the great minds of the past, when he was not confronting the mysteries of the future. In that ordinary medium-sized body was a captive eagle. Between the four walls of the house, its view limited by the shrubs and flowers in the garden, Melchior would forget time and eliminate space, living the retrospective or prophetic life—the sweet, mysterious, voluptuous pleasure of solitary beings. Melchior *was* a solitary man; in spite of his social relationships, which he cultivated, he loved above all else the time he spent apart from other human beings. During such hours, which were the greater part of his time, he would read or meditate, forgetting, or indifferent to, the things of his own century. On this occasion he was reading. Seeing Estacio's form loom in the doorway, he frowned but received him affably.

"I have interrupted you," said Estacio, "but I had to."

Melchior laid his book on the round table in the center of the room, marking the place with an old print. Then they sat down near one of the side windows. Estacio could not immediately bring himself to tell the reason he had come; but from his very hesitation Melchior deduced what it was.

"Had to?" repeated the priest.

"It concerns Helena. I know you are our friend. I have confidence in your opinions and discretion. Out of a desire for my family's happiness, you have sought to facilitate the marriage between Helena and Mendonça . . ."

"Counting on your approval," added the priest.

"I hesitate to give it."

"Why?"

Estacio explained that Helena had no inclination toward this intended husband. Melchior answered with the simple facts and said in conclusion, "It is true she does not love him ardently, but she accepts him, she has regard for him, she is halfway along the road to the happiness we ought to give her."

"There is one difficulty, Reverend Father. She loves another man."

Melchior grew white; he fixed on Estacio's face the penetrating eyes of a judge in a glance that was sharp and immovable. The young man's stern countenance did not change nor did he lower his eyes. "She loves another," he continued, "with a violent passion but without hope, a passion as real as it is mysterious. She alluded to it once or twice but I could never wrest any more from her. Just now, when I spoke to her about it, she turned aside the implication and the conversation. I know no more. I know, however, that she still loves him, and to marry in such circumstances gives rise to two difficulties, both equally grave: she deprives herself of the possibility of a happy union with the man she secretly loves, and she brings to her husband's house a feeling of regret and remorse. Does that seem to you something to be tolerated?"

"There is no remorse, no regret, where there is no hope," returned the priest. "Helena accepts Mendonça of her own free will, and I know her well enough to think it no longer possible for her to take back her word."

"Save for my consent."

"Naturally; but why would you refuse it?"

"Because I have not given up hope of discovering the person to whom Helena has given her heart. Perhaps she thinks impossible something that is only difficult. Besides, let us not forget that Helena is barely seventeen years old."

"Her seventeen is as good as twenty-five."

"Maybe so; but we should not accept lightly a condescension on her part, or her whim, or whatever other hidden motive prompts her to make this resolve."

"What could be her motive?"

"How should I know! Perhaps a suspicion that we would like to see her out of our house."

"Do not malign her; Helena has a perfect understanding and appreciation of the love and affection that surround her and of the high regard in which she is held. Your objections have no validity in the face of the declaration she herself made. Let us not complicate a simple, well-defined situation."

Melchior uttered these words in a gentle voice but in a firm manner. Estacio did not have the courage to answer them immediately. He returned to his first line of argument, then ventured a new objection. "Mendonça is a good-hearted fellow," he said, "but in my opinion he does not possess the qualities that should distinguish Helena's husband. He will never have the influence over her that a husband should have. With them the pyramid will be inverted, and the base of the conditions of marriage that assure domestic happiness will be destroyed. But there is a greater danger, that is, that he would come to lose his wife's respect. In that case, what would we be giving her? An apparent marriage but a real divorce."

The priest was not looking at him but was gazing out the window with doleful eyes and an impatient air. When he finished, Melchior looked directly at him with determination, saying the matter in hand was not to give Helena some specially endowed husband but the man she herself had chosen of her own free will, that it was incumbent upon them to see that the marriage take place without delay. Of course, as head of the family, Estacio could oppose the marriage or set conditions; but that would not be to Helena's interest or even to the interest of the family.

Estacio stood up when the priest finished speaking, walked through the room, silent and pensive. After a few seconds Melchior went to him. "Go tell your aunt the whole story," he said. "Give your consent to your sister. I will marry you both on the same day."

"All right," said Estacio, as if concluding an argument with himself, "I consent to Helena's marriage, but let us look for another husband. Mendonça, no; it must be someone else. Now that I am getting married, I will be having weekly at-homes; some young man will appear who is deserving of her, someone she can really love... That is my final decision."

## Chapter XIX

As Estacio uttered these words, Mendonça entered the chaplain's garden gate. Troubled by Estacio's coldness, he too had decided to have a talk with Melchior and ask his advice. Melchior was on the point of answering Estacio when he heard footsteps on the gravel of the garden walk. "Here comes the bridegroom," he said.

Estacio walked over to pick up his hat, reconsidered and sat down again at the round table. A copy of the Scriptures was lying there. He opened it at random, as it happened, to a page of Proverbs, and read this verse: "Whosoever would rid himself of his friend doth seek occasions for it, and he will be covered with infamy." Shamed, Estacio turned over the leaf. Mendonça came into the room. He had not counted on Estacio's being there but was glad to see that he was.

"Come in," said Melchior. "We have just been talking about your marriage."

Estacio cast a reproachful look at the priest. The priest did not see it; he was looking at Mendonça, who immediately answered him. "The very reason I am here. Since fortune has made you our confidant, I wish to constitute you my counselor and guide."

"I am also an advocate for your cause. Even now I was expounding its advantages."

Mendonça looked fixedly at his friend, and after a short pause, "Do you reject or accept the suitor?" he asked.

Caught between the devil and the deep, Estacio did not find a ready answer. He stared down at the open page of the holy book, afraid to meet the eyes of the other two. The silence was worse than an answer; neither the situation nor the persons permitted such a long pause. Estacio suddenly shut the book and stood up. "We were only discussing the advantages of marriage," he said.

"And what is your opinion?"

"It is my opinion that Helena is still a very young girl. But it is not only that, nor is that the main thing. After all, I am in favor of marriage. The main concern is your reputation."

"My reputation?"

"Helena might come to love you as you deserve; the truth is that she does not feel, up to now, a passion equal to yours. It was the reverend father who told me this. She has esteem for you, it is true, but esteem is the flower of reason, and I believe that the flower of sentiment is much more appropriate in the garden of matrimony..."

"There are a lot of flowers in that bunch of rhetoric of yours," interposed the priest kindly. "Let us speak in plain, simple language. Do not take literally what this philosopher says," he went on, turning to Mendonça. "He loves you both and wants to see you both happy. It is his very zeal that makes him speak in this way. In a word, he desires that you, sir, conquer her heart after a formal campaign..."

Mendonça answered the chaplain with a pallid smile that slightly raised the points of his moustache; immediately after, he withdrew into a cool reticence. His face had become downcast and thoughtful: Estacio's phrase had struck home. Disposed to accept Helena's esteem and friendship with the hope of converting that small dowry into a considerable capital, the thought had not occurred to him that to other eyes it might appear that his exclusive object was the girl's wealth. Estacio had torn the veil that covered that possibility. A single word had demolished the illusion of the last few days.

"Come," said the priest, "embrace as brothers."

Neither moved. Melchior sensed the gravity of the situation; he saw his efforts wasted, the union they had agreed to annulled, a chasm sprung between the two friends, Helena's future uncertain. He intervened once more with gentle words, which they both listened to without interrupting. When he finished, Mendonça spoke. "Estacio is right," he said, "my reputation will suffer, for someone will be sure to suggest that the marriage was arranged without regard for Dona Helena's preferences. *She* will release me from our agreement in exchange for her given word, which I now restore to her." The words came forth sadly, but without hesitation or weakness.

Estacio looked at him and felt something like remorse. An inner voice seemed to be saying to him: "Sleepwalker, open your eyes, see what you are doing; your embrace is a hangman's noose, your scruples make you odious; your solicitude is worse than angry rage." He saw Mendonça bow to the priest, and caught his arm to detain him. "Where are you going?" he asked.

"Where my honor takes me," Mendonça replied simply.

"Poor boys!" exclaimed the priest. "You are two rash fools, nothing more: one searching for objections to what his sister considered a noble and frank resolution; the other light-heartedly breaks a promise made in the presence of God's priest. Rash fools, did I say? You are worse than that. You are two madmen. Well! As I am the only one of us in his right mind, and am consequently in authority, I say to the one, 'Do not give up and leave here with disappointed hopes.' To the other I say, 'You must not refuse the assent that I beg of you in the name of your dead father'."

A shudder went through Estacio. Mendonça remained cold and distant. The weapon was a valiant one but the blow exceeded what was called for. Melchior knew it when he saw Estacio hold out his hand to his friend, and the friend take it with icy dignity.

Had Estacio been counting on this repulse by her suitor? What is certain is that he said to him without the least shadow of hesitation: "My zeal was perhaps excessive; my intention is good and without reservation. What can I wish but to see those close to me happy? Love each other; it will be the crowning glory of my aspirations. Do you promise to make her happy?"

"No. I promise nothing," said Mendonça. "The marriage is no longer possible. You have opened my eyes. I don't hold it against you. My loss is great, to be sure, but I shall not be exposed to the tongues of the malicious."

He picked up his hat and prepared to leave in spite of Melchior, who intervened, trying to bring him round to a willingness for reconciliation. The priest did not insist; he saw in the young man's face an honorable, firm resolve which was impossible to bend at the moment. When Mendonça held out his hand to him in farewell, he pressed it tenderly and with hope. Estacio tried to detain him; it was no use. Mendonça left them, without rancor but also without regret. His heart bled, but his conscience was at peace.

Melchior saw him to the door, and when he went out, turned to face inside, folded his arms, and fixed his gaze on Estacio. The young man averted his eyes. "Did you see that?" asked the priest. "I do not know what you may decide to do, but I promise you that I shall be like Mohammed — God pardon me! — even though I may see the sun on my right hand and the moon on my left, I will not abandon my purpose. Go talk with your family; leave me a few moments with my breviary."

Estacio could not oppose the holy father's ultimatum; he could not find a word to say to him. He left there bewildered, disconsolate, full of rage. In the street and in the chácara, he kept thinking of the scene of the last hour and he seemed to be piecing together a dream. He did not recognize himself, he prodded his intellect, he called to his aid all the forces of reality; he looked at the ground as if suspecting that he was treading clouds of mist. When reason finally found a footing among all those confused recollections, he saw clearly the result of his actions: he had lost a friend of many years, he had abdicated as head of the family, at least so far as his sister's marriage was concerned. If she should thank him for his opposition, he would consider himself well repaid for it all. Was it not for her benefit that he had schemed? This thought raised his spirits; if he should have her approval the rest would matter little to him.

Helena listened to his faithful account of what had taken place at Melchior's house. She listened deeply moved. When he finished, she condemned all that he had done. "Mendonça is now forbidden fruit," she added in conclusion, "I am beginning to love him. If you persist in urging me to give up the marriage, I shall adore him."

"So, we arrive at caprice!" he exclaimed. "The true basis of a woman's heart!"

Helena smiled and turned from him. She went up to her room, took her pen and wrote a short note. The ink was dry before the two tears that fell on the paper were, but the tears also dried. Before sealing the note she went down to show it to her brother.

When she entered the study Estacio was on the point of going to talk to her. He had made a decision. Inasmuch as his sister looked with favor upon the marriage, there was nothing else to do but approve it and see her married. They met in the doorway; Estacio went back inside. "Helena," said he, "what you want shall be done."

"You consent?"

He nodded.

"It will not be enough," she replied. "Mendonça will not come back here after what has taken place. I beg you to send him this note."

Estacio opened the note. It contained these few words: "Come to Andarahy today; my heart begs it of you, our happiness demands it." Estacio took five minutes to read the two lines; he read what was written there and what was not written. Helena was disarming Mendonça of his scruples, taking from the proposed union all suspicion of interest. He read and slowly folded the paper.

"Do you approve?" she asked.

"And so," he said sadly, "your happiness demands that

this man come here, that you marry him and abandon us? Our family is not enough for you? our aunt's love? *my* love? all this is not enough? Are these months of sweet intimacy to be forgotten in a single instant? sacrificed at the feet of the first man that it pleases you to choose and follow? On the day you came into this house there entered with you a ray of new light, a something we lacked that you brought with you; our family became complete; our hearts received that final wonderful feeling. We thought it would last forever, but it was ephemeral. O Helena, better not to have come!"

Helena tried to answer; her voice stuck in her throat and the words returned to her heart. She pointed to the note as if again begging him to send it.

In the afternoon Melchior came to them, calm and resolute, to strike the decisive blow. Estacio yielded before the priest could say a word. "Reverend Father," he said as soon as he caught sight of him, "reflection has won me over. Let your wishes, the wishes of all be gratified."

"You speak from the heart?"

"From the heart."

"Well then," continued the priest, "go all the way. I am minister of a religion that condemns pride. It is no dishonor to cure a friend's wounds; go speak with your friend and bring him to this house as a brother."

"I'll go tomorrow."

"No, go today."

Night was falling. Estacio went up to dress. Not having sent Helena's note, he put it in his pocket with the idea of handing it to Mendonça himself. Afterward he took it out and reread it; having reread it, he made as if to tear it in two but restrained himself and passed it once more beneath his eyes. But, his hand like an indiscreet moth seemed attracted by the light; it resisted; it resisted for some time; finally it approached the note to the candle and burned it.

## Chapter XX

Estacio's visit caused Mendonça no surprise; he was expecting it with the confidence of an open-hearted nature incapable of hatred. He could not believe that a friend of so many years would sleep on the unjust act of a minute; but the friend did. It was the next morning when Estacio called on Helena's suitor. He entered Mendonça's house in a natural manner, without effusiveness but not with an air of indifference either. The meeting was brief but cordial. They both conducted themselves with friendly dignity. Estacio explained his scruples, declaring he rejoiced in the alliance. His joy may have existed; its manifestation, however, was thin and dry. There was more warmth and effusiveness when he begged him to make a happy life for his sister.

"It will cause me eternal remorse if Helena should fall on misfortune. We did not share the same cradle, we passed our childhood under different roofs, we did not learn to speak from the lips of the same mother. It matters little; not for these reasons do I love her any the less. My father entrusted her to our love and she responded in kind to the feeling which his last wish laid upon us."

Mendonça made no reply; he had reflected during the night upon Estacio's remark of the day before, a remark that might well be made, or thought, by others, perhaps by everyone as soon as they learned of his marriage. Helena would come to love him perhaps; but now she would bring to his house the key of independence. He drew back in refusal.

When Father Melchior learned of it, he could not repress a gesture of admiration; but if he applauded the scruple he did not approve the decision, which would ruin everything. "You will never stop the mouths of the malicious," he said, "they will find a way to poison your generosity."

"Wait a moment!" retorted the young man. "What you mention is a lesser danger. If I marry they will say I have made a profitable deal. Perhaps her family will think the same; perhaps she herself will think so."

Helena heard of her suitor's misgivings and of the decision which his heart seemed to prompt. She asked him if it was true. He assured her that it was. She looked at him for a long time without saying a word; then she grasped his hands and pressed them warmly; he remained firm.

There may have been a bit of pretension in his disinterestedness. The lady perceived it; not for that reason did she cease to believe in his sincerity. She tried to dissuade him; and although she accomplished nothing in the first moments, she was sure she would win out in the end. Her eyes were bound to be more clever and fortunate than a priest's lips. That is what she told the chaplain. "I am making it my business to bring about the marriage," she added in conclusion.

"Determined to use any stratagem?"

"All of them."

"But if he persists . . ."

"I will conquer him by one means or another. A lady who wants to be a bride has the strength of an army; I am an army."

"Very good! And yet, your family position . . ."

"Oh! If it comes to that I will relinquish the inheritance."

"You would do that?"

"Would I? I long to do it," she retorted with vehemence. And she added more quietly, "I will not have the slightest speck of suspicion fall on the man of my choice."

Such was the situation two days after Estacio's return home. The marriage was now taken for granted. Mendonça's resistance had given way before Helena's disinterested attitude. Dona Ursula approved it all in a burst of effusive love—knowing nothing of the uncertainties and contradictions of the last two days.

That night Estacio wrote to Cantagallo, giving news of

himself. Of Helena's marriage he said little, almost nothing. He was dissatisfied with the whole thing, as much with what he himself had done and said to no avail, as with the outcome. He had succeeded neither in mounting an effective opposition nor in yielding at the right moment.

Although it was late, sleep stubbornly fled from him and he was still awake long after midnight. Busy no doubt in lulling to rest less sensitive organisms and less complicated existences, the god paid him but a short visit. Around five Estacio awoke and got up. The morning was cool; the household was mostly asleep. He went downstairs; the only slave he found stirring made him a cup of coffee. Since the papers had not yet come, he drank it without the customary perusal of them.

Who can say by what slender threads the events of a man's life are strung together. Estacio happened to hear the distant sound of a shot, some hunter perhaps. This conjecture gave him the idea of going hunting. He fetched his gun, provided himself powder and lead, and sallied forth.

If his skill in general was not very great, it seemed to be greatly diminished that morning, either because his hand was less steady or because his eyesight was less keen. He walked for a long time without remembering the reason he had come out, absorbed, his thoughts far from the place and everything around him. He made several attempts at shooting. When he grew weary of his fruitless ramble, he consulted his watch and saw it was getting late. His arm was tired from carrying the gun; only then did he notice that he had not brought a page along. He turned to go back. Spying an orchid, he picked it to give to Helena as a first wedding present. Then he started down the road home.

With his gun under his arm, his eyes on the ground, he descended slowly in spite of its being late. The one time he raised his eyes, he saw a strange thing that made him check his step. A little further down the road there came from behind an old house Helena's page leading the mule and the mare. Estacio did not know what to make of it. Yielding to an impulse he could not control he jumped over a thorn hedge and crouched to see the rest.

The rest was not long in coming. Helena's form appeared at the front door. After looking cautiously to one side and the other, she came out and mounted the mare; the page climbed astride the mule, and the two went off down the road at a trot.

Estacio felt a mist before his eyes; at the same time he grasped the first thing that came to hand; it was the thorn hedge. The pain made him return to his senses; his hand was bloodied. Helena and the page were riding off in the distance. As soon as he saw them disappear, he jumped back on the highway. Without resolve or plan, he walked toward the house he had seen his sister come out of. It was the one with the little blue flag that Helena had waved to from a distance some months before, and had not neglected to reproduce in the landscape she had given her brother on his birthday. These circumstances, hitherto of no importance, now appeared to him as so many counts in a bill of indictment.

The house looked even older than the first time he had seen it; the mortar of the walls and columns had begun to chip off and lay bare the brick skeleton here and there. Some wretched plants straggled up to its walls and covered the damp, uneven ground with discolored foliage. Below one of the windows was a wooden bench, dried and cracked by time and with edges rounded smooth from long use. Everything breathed want and feeble old age.

"No," Estacio said to himself, "this is not the secret hideaway of a bandit Romeo. It is the home of some poor family whom Helena's thoughtful charity comes to comfort from time to time."

This solution of the enigma seemed so natural that he

resolved to stop halfway in the adventure, and even retreated a few steps. But suspicion is the tapeworm of the mind; you cannot kill it as long as its head remains. Estacio felt an overpowering desire to find out what this thing was, and he retraced his steps. In order to get into the house he had to have a motive, or a pretext. He wracked his brain; the adventure had supplied him with the best possible one. He glanced at his bloodied hand and went to knock at the door.

## Chapter XXI

Estacio waited. In a few moments a man came to open the door. It was the same one he had seen there one time before. There was a half minute of silence between them, during which Estacio did not think to say what he wanted, or the unknown man to ask him who he was. They stood looking at each other.

Finally the master of the house spoke. "Is there something I can do for you?" he asked.

"A favor," answered Estacio, showing him his injured hand. "I was about to fall just now and to stop myself caught hold of a thorn hedge and injured myself as you see. Could you give me a little water to wash off this blood and . . ."

"Of course," interrupted the other. "Will you sit there on the bench, or, if you prefer, come inside . . . It will be better to come in the house," he concluded, throwing wide the door.

At any other time, Estacio would have refused the invitation. The spectacle of poverty was repugnant to his eyes, steeped as they were in abundance. Now, however, he burned to possess the key to the enigma. He went inside.

The stranger opened one of the windows to give more light, offered his guest the best chair, and left him for a moment to go into another room.

Estacio was then able to hastily examine the room in which he found himself. It was small and dark. The wall, covered with size of a long time back, bore all the marks of age; originally a single color, the paint now presented a sad, unpleasant variety. Here mildew, there a crack, yonder the rent caused by a piece of furniture, every accident of time or wear gave those four walls the aspect of a refuge for bad luck. There was little furniture and it was old, shabby, and ill-matched. Five or six chairs, not all of them whole, a round table, a chest of drawers, a cane-bottomed settee, a sideboard with two glass chimneys on brass candlesticks, on the table a porcelain vase with flowers, and on the wall two little pictures covered with dingy silk gauze—such were the furnishings of the room. The only thing with an air of life was the vase of flowers. They were fresh, gathered perhaps that very morning. When Estacio's eye fell on them he started: he thought he recognized an acacia that grew on his chácara. When suspicion germinates in the mind the least incident assumes a decisive aspect. Estacio felt a chill.

His host returned carrying a basin in his hands and over his arm a towel whose snowy whiteness contrasted strangely with the color of the wall and the senile aspect of the house in general. Estacio stood up.

"Don't get up," said the stranger.

"I am perfectly all right."

"In that case, be so kind as to come to the window." He set the basin on the window ledge and started to wash his guest's hand, but his guest would not permit it. "At least," said his host, "you must allow me to wipe it off. I understand something of this kind of thing; unfortunately I do not have any proper medicine in the house to put on it."

Estacio accepted his offer. The man opened the towel

and carefully began the operation. Estacio was then enabled to examine him at will. He was a man of thirty-six to thirty-eight years of age, strong limbed, tall and well proportioned. His heavy dark brown hair fell almost to his shoulders. His eyes were large and in general quiet but they laughed when his lips smiled and for a passing moment were enlivened with an intense brilliance. There was about that head, except for the side whiskers, a sort of air of an Italian tenor. His full, strong chest extended between broad shoulders, and through the opening of his shirt, which was loosely closed by a kerchief at the base of his neck, Estacio could see its white skin and hard musculature. His clothes were ragged but clean: a white jacket, jean trousers, and vest of buff-colored drill. The shabby, ill-assorted clothes did not diminish the masculine beauty of his person; they merely revealed his lack of means.

When he finished cleansing Estacio's scratches—they were little more than that—he suggested fetching a piece of cloth for a bandage. Estacio with his other hand and his teeth tore the handkerchief he had with him, and the master of the house completed the summary treatment. "There!" said he. "If you have some appropriate medicine at home it will be best to apply it. Every caution is little enough; it is well to avoid an inflammation."

"Thank you," Estacio answered. "Really, I have given you a lot of trouble, needlessly perhaps..."

"Why do you say that?"

"I could have done all this when I got home."

"You live nearby?"

"A piece down the road."

"It was best to take care of it right away. No precaution is too great for anything in life."

"A prudent maxim," observed Estacio, trying to smile.

"Learned only too late, if a man does not have it in his blood," the other replied with a sigh.

It was difficult to prolong the conversation without

being indiscreet or talkative. The favor had been done, the subject exhausted. All that remained was to express thanks, say goodbye, and leave. Estacio, however, had need of more time; he wanted to wrest from this man some word less indifferent to their situation, or to become acquainted, if possible, with his character and habits. There was, perhaps, a way of doing this; he could counterfeit an identity not his, assume manners foreign to his nature, grasp the occasion wherever it offered a hold. This was the course Estacio determined upon, trusting the rest to chance. He went back to the chair and sat down. "May I rest for a bit? I am terribly tired."

"Not from what you bagged today," said the stranger with a laugh.

"Yes, I come back empty-handed. I never was a good shot, and yet I have a mania for birding."

"Isn't that the failing of many other people, on a higher level of things? I myself was a victim of just such a human failing."

"Ah!" exclaimed Estacio with a certain interrogative intonation.

His host smiled slightly, but the guest's curiosity did not appear to bother him. Perhaps he was longing for this very thing. "It is true," said he. "I owe my present poverty to the mistake of persisting in things alien to my nature and my talents, alien, even totally contrary..."

"You must forgive me," interrupted Estacio with an air of obtrusive familiarity that was not habitual with him, "I believe that a strong, young, intelligent man has no right to sink into penury."

"Your remark," said the man, smiling, "has the aroma of the chocolate that you drank, no doubt, this morning, sir, before going out to hunt. I presume you are wealthy. It is impossible for those in easy circumstances to comprehend the struggles of the poor; and the maxim that every man can with effort arrive at the same brilliant result will always appear as a great truth to the person carving a turkey . . . Well, this is not the way it is. There are exceptions. In the actual affairs of this world, man is not as free as you suppose; and a thing some call fate, others coincidence, and that *we* have baptized with the genuine Brazilian name 'caiporismo' prevents many from ever seeing the fruits of their most Herculean labors. Caesar and his luck! The whole of human wisdom is contained in those four words."

The stranger uttered all this with the most simple and natural air in the world and with a facility in speaking that Estacio could scarcely have imagined to be his. Was he acting a part, or was it a genuine expression of the truth? Estacio looked hard at him, as if to penetrate his thought. At the same time, he heard an indistinct noise in the part of the house beyond the sitting room. He turned his head in startled distrust. A door opened and there appeared an old negro woman with a tray in her hands. She stopped midway.

"Place it on the table," said her master. "It is my breakfast," he added, turning to Estacio, "a spare healthful breakfast. May I venture to offer you a share of it?"

Estacio made a gesture of refusal and prepared to leave.

"Already? It was not my intention to dismiss you; I can breakfast and talk at the same time. I live such a solitary life that the presence of another person is a delightful diversion . . . ."

Estacio accepted without hesitation, sat down at the table facing the man, and assisted at his breakfast, which could not have been more meager: a roll, two wafers of hard cheese, and a large cup of coffee. What was more significant was the man's contentment and the frankness with which he displayed the simplicity of his habits to the eyes of a stranger.

"It is not a meal fit for a king," said he, "but it satisfies a stomach that has no hope of more. This is my drawing room, and dining room; the kitchen is adjoining; outside are a dozen feet of backyard, and over there beyond the yard...the infinity of human indifference." After a silence, he added: "No, I am wrong. I do not always encounter indifference. My work gives me no more than my poor daily bread, but I have some joys in the midst of my perpetual Lent, and these I receive from hands that are charitable and pure."

Saying this, he drained his cup, leaned back in his chair, and looked his guest full in the face. Estacio reflected upon these last words, and a ray of light broke through the cloud that darkened his face. The two men seemed to be interrogating each other. The counselor's son took a cigar out of his pocket and offered it to the cottager.

"Thank you, no," said the latter.

"Don't you smoke?"

"I've had one; I now economize this vice. My digestion is none the worse for it."

"Do you live alone?"

"Yes."

"You have no family?"

"None."

"You must think me strangely inquisitive..."

"No. I suppose you have an honorable and logical reason for your curiosity."

"You are right. You, sir, inspire me with a sympathetic fellow feeling. And if *I* should happen to know a pair of those pure hands that correct fortune's errors for you..."

"You would give me, with them as intermediary, your mite of alms?"

"If it would not offend you..."

"It would not offend me, but I would refuse it if I knew; and I earnestly beg you not to do it in secret..."

Estacio made a gesture of assent.

"It is not pride," continued his host. "It is a remnant of decency which poverty has not yet taken from me. I did you a slight service, a simple neighborly act. . . . It would appear that you, sir, would be paying me for it with a charitable gift. The gift would be less than spontaneous on your part and less than agreeable to me. *Agreeable* does not express my whole idea; but you, sir, will readily understand what I mean."

"You misunderstand me; my mite would not be in the specie to which you allude, sir. I have friends and a certain amount of influence. I could arrange a better position for you . . ."

The stranger reflected a moment.

"You would accept?"

"I am thinking of a way to refuse. Gold is what gold buys. It would be an eternal humiliation for me to owe betterment of my lot to the performance of a charitable duty."

"I no longer wonder that you lead a life of poverty."

"Excessive scruples, eh? . . ."

"Beyond all reason!"

"Better more than less."

"Better neither more nor less but just the right amount."

"The amount varies according to the moral requirements of each individual. But I myself, who am telling you this, did not always have this intractable virtue, and possibly at times I was weak . . ." The man's brow darkened; his voice died on his lips and his eyes had the dulled look of great mental concentration. It was the moment to put the direct question to him or leave. Estacio chose the latter alternative.

"I will detain you no longer," said his host when the young gentleman rose to take his leave. "It is late, and your mother may perhaps be worried . . ."

Estacio limited himself to looking him full in the face and saying, "If you decide to rid yourself of your scruples sometime, send to me. My house is known throughout Andarahy as Counselor Valle's house . . ."

The stranger, on whose face Estacio had expected to see

some sign of discomposure or surprise, remained impassive and smiling; then he bowed in acknowledgment, and, as Estacio was slow in holding out his hand, *he* put his hands in his pockets.

"Perhaps we shall see each other again," said Estacio, already outside the door.

"Yes?"

"I sometimes ride this way."

"I am not always at home; but even when I am I keep the doors shut. Whenever you would like to stop and rest, knock. It is a poor house but you will find it a friendly one."

Estacio rapidly moved off. It was ten o'clock and the sun was getting hot; he did not notice the sun nor the time. Like the Florentine who lost his way, he found himself in a dark wood at an equal distance from the right path and the fatal gate where he feared to be stripped of all hope. He knew nothing for certain, he could make no conjectures; all was fresh doubts and oscillations. The man with whom he had been talking seemed to be sincere; his poverty was authentic, and the note of melancholy that sometimes made his words trail off into silence was perceptible. But where did reality cease and appearance begin? Had he been dealing with an unlucky wretch or with a hypocrite? Estacio recalled all the incidents of the morning and all the unknown man's words; they were just so many question marks, suspect and unanswered. He repelled with horror the idea of wrong; it was hard for him to accept the idea of good; and the worst of his torments—doubt—held him and shook him in its feline grip. The sun and his mental agitation brought out pearls of sweat on his forehead; his rapid movement combined with the violence of his emotion made him gasp for breath. He did not see the objects he passed nor the people who went by him; he continued blind and deaf until the shock of reality should arouse him.

He finally arrived home. He gave his gun to the slave at

the gate. His overlong absence had caused some uneasiness in the household. As soon as the two ladies learned of his return, they ran to greet him, Dona Ursula remaining at a window, Helena going halfway down the veranda steps. The sudden apparition of the girl, the joy and love that seemed to impel her, the perfect ingenuousness of her gestures, all produced the needed reaction, reaction of an instant but salutary, for his emotional crisis had been violent beyond endurance. Estacio grasped Helena's hands with force. A subtle fluid coursed through her very being and that rapid instant had all the sweetness of a reconciliation.

Estacio had counted on retiring to his room in order to put his ideas in order, compare them, and extract at least a conjecture from them, verify it or disprove it. But neither his aunt nor his sister had breakfasted, waiting for him to join them, and he was obliged to do so, to satisfy a need that he did not feel. During breakfast he tried to observe Helena closely, an idle effort, because if her face betrayed anything on that occasion it was delight in her family. She served both Estacio and Dona Ursula with her own hands, deftly dividing her loving attentions, and her grace, between them. In her eyes one seemed to read ignorance of evil, and her smile was that of an unblemished soul. Could he attribute corruption and hypocrisy to this creature of seventeen years? Estacio blushed at the idea; he felt a remorse that dizzied him.

But, breakfast over, the company separated and the young man withdrew to his study. Then, the vision absent, suspicion returned. Estacio tried to master the situation. He would not go so far as to suppose a complete perversion of feeling in Helena; the worst wrongdoing he could attribute to her was a culpable thoughtlessness. If, instead of a thoughtless act, it was a simple stratagem for charity, she nonetheless deserved a warning; but purity of intention would save everything, and the family's peace no less than its dignity would be restored intact. Estacio examined one by one the bits of evidence for culpability and for innocence; he searched with all sincerity for elements of proof; he did not overlook a single inductive argument. He spent a long time at this task without appreciable result, because not only was the sentence difficult to formulate but also the judge was incompetent to make a decision.

Just before dinner time, Estacio, who had not left his study all day, went to one of its windows and saw crossing the chácara the most insignificant figure in the whole enigma, insignificant and important at the same time, Helena's page. The boy appeared as a new idea to Estacio, who till that moment had not once given him a thought. *He* was the confidant and the accomplice. On seeing him, Estacio recalled that Helena had once asked him for the slave's liberty. A threat roared in his heart but his anger gave way to anguish and he felt something like a tear on his cheek. At the same moment his eyes were blindfolded by a pair of hands.

## Chapter XXII

No great effort was needed to guess the fair owner of those hands. With *his* hands he took away Helena's, securing her wrists in such a way as to draw from her a faint cry of pain. He turned and saw his sister, who said to him in a tone of merry reproach, "You are very mean! You paid me for a caress with a rough squeeze. Just you wait and see if I ever give you another. I came to look for you because you haven't deigned to give us even a glimpse of your charming presence this whole day... You hurt me!" she added, looking at her wrists. "But my fingers are wet; would... could you be... what is it? What happened?"

Estacio listened to his sister with downcast, anxious look and did not answer her, only went on looking at her as if trying to read in her expression the answer to the puzzle that bewildered him. Helena insisted, frightened and distressed. When she tried to lay hold of his hands he pulled away from her and walked to the opposite wall, took down the drawing she had given him on his birthday, and went up to her.

"What is it?" she repeated in amazement.

Estacio's only reply was to place his finger on the mysterious house reproduced in the landscape. Helena looked alternately at the drawing and at her brother. His questioning, imperious expression drew her attention to the spot indicated by his finger. Suddenly she grew white; her lips trembled as if murmuring something, but intention spoke so low that it did not reach utterance. They remained so for several seconds. Their anguish could be read in both their faces. To hide *her* pain Helena covered her eyes with her hands. The gesture was eloquent. Estacio hurled the picture from him with an angry gesture. Helena rushed out into the hall.

Dona Ursula was waiting dinner for them. When they did not appear, she went to Estacio's study. The door was open. She went in and found him seated in a big easy chair, holding a handkerchief to his face; he appeared to be sobbing. His aunt ran to him with all the speed her years permitted. Estacio did not hear her come in; he did not know she was there until she pulled his hands away from his eyes. Her astonishment was indescribable, especially when Estacio stood up and threw himself into her arms, crying, "What a cursed fatality!"

"But... what is?... explain..."

With the determined gesture of a man ashamed of an act of weakness, Estacio wiped away the tears of an intense spell of weeping. The outburst had calmed his spirits; he could finally be a man, and there was need that he be one.

Dona Ursula begged and commanded him to tell her the reason for the incomprehensible state of distress she had found him in. He refused to say what it was. "You will know everything tomorrow, or later on today. Now, the only thing I could tell you would be an enigma, and I know what that has cost *me*. A few hours more and I shall want your advice and support."

Dona Ursula resigned herself to waiting. When she returned to the dining room she found Helena had sent word that she felt suddenly indisposed and begged to be excused for that afternoon and evening. Dona Ursula suspected at once that Helena's message had some relation to Estacio's distress, and she ran to her niece's room. She found her half reclined on the bed with her face in the pillow, her body still and corpselike. Hearing Dona Ursula's step, she raised her head. She was pale and dispirited, but there had been no tears. Her grief, if she had suffered any, and she had, seemed turned to stone. The only thing alive in her girlish figure was her eyes; they had not lost their natural brilliance. She raised them fearfully and embraced her aunt with a look of supplication and love. Dona Ursula took her hands in hers, silently regarded her, and murmured, "Tell me everything."

"You will soon know!" she sighed.

"Don't you trust your aunt?"

Helena rose and threw her arms around Dona Ursula. Two tears welled in her eyes; they were the first she had shed during that whole half-hour. Then she tenderly kissed Dona Ursula's hands. "You may receive these kisses," said she, "an angel's are not more pure."

Those were the last words Dona Ursula could wrest from her; she withdrew into the silence in which the aunt had found her. Dona Ursula left the room and went to find her nephew. He was on his way to the dining room. "Let us sit down to dinner," he said. "It's not proper for the slaves to know of our difficulties . . ."

Dona Ursula described the state she had found Helena in and the words she had exchanged with her. Estacio listened without any sign of sympathy. Dinner was an empty show, a means of deceiving the slaves' perspicacity; they, however, were not taken in. They knew perfectly well that some concealed happening occupied their masters' thought and held it in suspense. Delicacies returned to the kitchen almost untouched; remarks were exchanged with effort between old mistress and young master. The cause of it surely was Nhanhan Helena.

Estacio gave orders that all callers be told the family was not at home. The only exception was Father Melchior; he wrote to him requesting him to come see them.

"I cannot wait till tomorrow," said Dona Ursula. "If you have to reveal something to a stranger, why not to me first? Tell me what it is. I can't bear to see Helena suffer; I want to comfort her and cheer her."

"What I have to tell is a long, sad story," returned Estacio, "but if you wish to hear it now, I beg you to wait at least until Father Melchior comes. I could not tell the same things over twice; it would be turning the knife in the wound."

Dona Ursula's curiosity was increased by these half-words of her nephew's; but she had to wait perforce and she waited. She went back to Helena's room. As the door was closed, she peeked through the keyhole. Helena was writing. This new circumstance had the effect of complicating Dona Ursula's impressions.

"Helena is shut up in her room, and she is writing," she told her nephew.

"Naturally," he replied dully.

Father Melchior did not delay in responding to Estacio's appeal; his note was urgent and the handwriting shaky and uneven. Something serious must have happened. The priest's conjecture was correct, as we know; he too found it so not much later in the family's mournful aspect and the anxiety with which he was awaited. All three retired to an inner room.

"Helena?" asked Melchior.

"She is what we are here to speak about," answered Estacio.

To relate what had taken place on that fatal morning was easier to plan than execute. When it came to revealing the situation and its attendant circumstances, Estacio felt that his rebellious tongue was not obeying his intention. He found himself in a domestic court, and what had been till then an inner conflict between love and honor must now be reduced to a formal indictment, clear, cold, and firm. Innocent or guilty, Helena appeared to him at that moment a memory of happy hours, a tender recollection that present or future events could only render more full of regret and longing but would never destroy, because that is the mysterious privilege of the past. Nevertheless he fought against himself and, although with difficulty, related in detail and accurately what had passed since morning.

Dona Ursula's heart was not formed for such sensitive revelations. From the very beginning of the conversation she felt the bewilderment that great blows cause. She had expected of course a misfortune for Helena, an episode in her former family life, something that would provoke pity without lessening their respect for her. Exactly the opposite had occurred. Respect was impossible and pity became little more than probable. "No! It's impossible," she cried a few moments later, when reason, obscured by the blow, could regain some of its light. "No! I have just seen her; I felt her tears on my face, I heard her speak words that only innocence could utter. And, besides, her blameless life here, almost a year in our family and not a single thing to reproach her with, and the refinement of her sentiments . . . I cannot believe that what you say . . . No! poor Helena! Let us send for her; she will explain everything. Let us question Vicente."

A gesture on the part of the two men showed that neither of them judged this last expedient an honorable one for getting at the truth.

Dona Ursula was prostrated; she recalled her apprehensions of that first day, and recoiled in horror from the idea of being proven correct. Estacio sat facing her in an old overstuffed chair, his elbows sunk in its arms and his hands dejectedly holding his burning temples, his whole soul going over and over his grief and pain.

Only one of the three attained to dignity in the situation. Melchior felt no less astonishment than Helena's two relatives, nor did he feel the blow less; but he rose above one and the other; he was able to triumph over his feelings and keep his reason clear, cold, and penetrating. He understood that those two lacerated hearts had not the strength to act. The principal action was to be his; he did not shirk the responsibility. He saw in a flash the possible extension of the evil, the disunion of the family, the despair of the moment, hatreds on the following days, indelible bitterness, and, perhaps, indelible regrets and longing. Even this picture did not frighten him, but he did not accept it without examination. Melchior was not wont to either condemn or absolve; he would wait and hope. He belonged to the number of those simple, virtuous men for whom vice is a rare exception; a sincere, open nature, it was hard for him to believe in hypocrisy. While Estacio continued silent and pensive, and Dona Ursula, now seated, now on her feet, punctuated the silence with cries of painful grief, Melchior observed them and reflected. Finally he spoke these words of encouragement: "Be calm, Dona Ursula. The truth is bound to come out and we have no certainty that it will be what we now suppose. In any case, let us not anticipate trouble. It would mean suffering twice over. There will be plenty of time for weeping." He got up. "One must shake off despair," he added, turning to Estacio. "It is the moment for vigorous action. Above all, it is best for the present to keep a close mouth on this matter; our mutterings would give rise to common gossip and idle comment. In this confused affair I will take the post that is my due, if you do not object . . ."

"Oh!" exclaimed Estacio.

"I wish you both to understand here and now that if honor demands one thing, charity demands another, and it is our strict duty to reconcile them. No hatreds; pardon or forget."

"But, Reverend Father, what do you think?" Dona Ursula asked anxiously.

"Dona Ursula," replied the priest, "now is the time for reason to speak and exert itself; feeling must withdraw and wait. I shall look well into the matter and prescribe the required remedy. Maybe we are fighting shadows; who knows? a question of a mistake, of appearance . . ."

"Oh!" interposed Estacio, "she confessed to everything! I saw the look of guilt in her eyes. But, after all, I am ready for anything you suggest," he continued, rising. "Weren't you one of my father's best friends? Aren't you still our friend? Help us, counsel us; we will do what you think best. Under the present circumstances neither of us has presence of mind capable of gathering the elements of proof, sifting them, and coming to a decision. That is your role." He was interrupted by a slave bringing him a letter; it was from Dr. Camargo: Eugenia's godmother had passed away and he would be back in Rio de Janeiro within a few days. It was the worst possible moment for his coming. Estacio could not repress a gesture of annoyance. The priest, informed of the substance of the letter, remarked that there would be no inconvenience in Camargo's return if the matter which troubled them was handled without delay.

"Dona Ursula," he continued, "leave us alone for a few moments. Remain calm; trust in God, and see that you don't do anything that will make people suspect what is going on in this house."

As soon as Dona Ursula left the room, Melchior closed the door. Estacio sat down again, prepared to listen to his chaplain. The latter took a few steps from the door to one of the windows. It was getting dark; Estacio lighted a candelabrum. Melchior sat down by him without saying a word to him or even turning his eyes in his direction. He was meditating, or debating with himself. His heavy, melancholy look betrayed an inner agitation. It was no longer the usual undisturbed placidity, reflection of a pure, religious conscience. If his conscience was the same, his heart was not, for it had come to grips with a new crisis. After ten minutes of profound silence between them, the priest spoke.

## Chapter XXIII

"Do you have courage? Can you be strong?" he asked.

"Yes."

"Do you believe in God?"

Estacio trembled and looked at the venerable priest without answering.

Melchior insisted: "Do you?"

"Your question . . ."

"Is less otiose than you think. It is not enough to assume that one believes. It is not enough to believe perfunctorily as one believes in the existence of a remote region of Asia where you never expect to set foot. The God I speak of is not only the sublime necessity of the mind which contents your philosophers; I speak to you of God the Creator and Remunerator, the God who reads the depths of our consciences, who gave us life and will give us death, and, beyond death, reward or punishment. Do you believe in him?"

"Yes."

"Well then . . . you have transgressed God's law and man's without knowing it. Your heart is a great unconscious offender; it is restless, it mutters, it rebels, it goes astray in the guise of an ill-expressed, ill-understood instinct. Evil pursues you, tempts you, envelops you in its hidden golden snares; you do not feel it nor see it; you will shrink from yourself in horror when you come face to face with it. God who reads you knows in his perfection that there is a thick veil between your heart and your conscience, separating them and preventing them from joining in a partnership of crime."

"Crime, Reverend Father?"

Melchior leaned over and looked hard at him, his eyes a cold polished mirror meant to reproduce the impression of what he was going to say. "Estacio," he said slowly and distinctly, "you are in love with your sister."

The look of mixed horror, amazement, and remorse with which Estacio heard this statement, showed the priest not only that he had hit upon the truth but also that he had just revealed it to the young lover. What Estacio's consciousness did not know, his heart knew but did not tell him until that solemn moment. Consciousness, groping in the dark, recoiled in terror as if to ward off the sudden light that blazed from the priest's words.

Estacio made no response. What response could he make? In what terms, in what human tongue could he express the strange, terrible commotion that shook his whole being? What thread of logic could tie together his broken, scattered ideas? He did not speak, he did not dare raise his eyes, he sat in a lifeless stupor. Melchior contemplated him some minutes silently and compassionately. The priest's eyes were those of an eagle for life's mysteries, but he had a dove's eyes for great misfortunes. In that breast below the virile masculine head was a woman's heart.

Estacio's dumbness finally came to an end. His body moved restlessly. His lips articulated some disconnected phrases, their sense vague; one might conclude that he did not believe in Melchior's revelation, the supposed feeling being so absurd and unnatural that it could be attributed only to bad instincts.

Melchior listened to him and smiled with satisfaction. Was this not the protest of an upright conscience? "Bad instincts, no," said he, "a deviation from social and religious law, but an unconscious deviation. Look into your heart, Estacio, search its innermost recesses and there you will find the deadly seed. Cast it out; that is the teaching of the Eternal Master. You never perceived it; temptation uses the serpent's cunning; it is as insinuating as calumny, as tenacious as suspicion. But I am the truth that confirms and the charity that consoles. I tell you not that you sinned but that you were on the brink of sinning and I hold out my hand to pull you back from the abyss."

"Reverend Father," murmured Estacio, whose heart felt the influence of Melchior's stern but gentle words.

"Do not speak," the priest continued. "To deny it is to lie; to confess it is idle. How did such a feeling come to be in your heart? Fortune decreed there should be no semblance of childhood between you nor a sharing of first years; in full-blown youth you were to enter, strangers unknown to each other, into a day-by-day intimacy. This was the root of the evil. Helena came upon your vision a grown woman, with all a woman's seductive qualities and still more with her own spiritual qualities, for nature and breeding had joined hands to make her original and superior. You were not aware of the slow transformation taking place within you, nor would you have been able to understand it. Saint Paul said: 'Unto the pure all things are pure.' You saw lawful affection in what was unlawful love; hence your jealousy, suspicion, demanding egotism with intent to draw Helena's soul away from all life's joys for the sole purpose of contemplating it yourself, alone, like a miser . . ."

As he listened to the priest, Estacio spelled out what was in his own heart, letter by letter, and clearly read what had been till then a closed book. His distress became still greater, his shame profound, his remorse intense. He stood up; as he did so, his eyes fell on the Counselor's portrait, which in the half-light seemed to eye his son with a questioning look. This circumstance completely disoriented him.

"No, Reverend Father," he cried, letting himself fall back in the chair. "It is impossible! What you have been saying is a bad dream. It's a tragic misunderstanding. It is impossible. I swear to you that it is impossible. It is true, I love her . . . I have loved her with a brother's love; but to forget myself, to foster in myself such an odious passion . . . Oh! It would be impossible!"

Melchior rose. After taking a half dozen steps he drew near Estacio, extended his right hand over his head and with his other hand raised Estacio's chin, obliging him to look at him. "I tell you that a poisonous herb has taken root in your heart. This is the cruel truth. There is an interconnection of feelings in man, sometimes inexplicable . . . Things grown in another clime when transplanted here alter or get mixed . . . But do you want to know the rest?"

"The rest?"

"Listen," continued the priest, sitting down again. "This poisonous plant sent forth a branch into Helena's chaste, virgin heart, and the same passion bound you both in its invisible tendrils. You did not see it, nor did she; but I saw it, I was the unhappy spectator of your terrible and pitiable situation. You are brother and sister, yet you love each other. Tragic poetry can turn the matter into a dramatic action for the stage, but what morality and religion condemn must not find refuge in the soul of an honest Christian man."

"Impossible! impossible!" cried Estacio. "But granted it be so why add the horror of such a revelation to our present difficulty?"

"Because the revelation explains the difficulty. Helena could not know that she loved you but she did. Well, a clandestine affair joined with this other incestuous, though unconscious, love would indicate a perversion in Helena that she cannot have; at her age it would be monstrous. Could Helena be such a monster? If she were I would despair of human nature. No, that house you saw her enter is surely a refuge of poverty; what she must be taking there is alms and pity."

A ray of hope shone in Estacio's face. The priest's reasoning was logical, and however perilous might be the situation revealed by him nothing better could now be desired: the family honor would remain intact. Estacio reflected a long time on what he had just heard. But hope was brief, although need for it was great.

"Is Helena still keeping to her room?" asked the priest.

Estacio made a slight sign in the affirmative.

"I will speak to her tomorrow; for today it is best to say nothing and keep everything quiet." Melchior withdrew into silence, as if still pondering something.

Estacio got up and began to pace slowly back and forth. From time to time he clutched his head in both hands; so much agitation, so many emotional shocks, would have bewildered a much hardier nature. Mystery enclosed him on all sides. He walked to the window, from there to the door, punctuating an inner meditation with a vigorous brandishing of an arm or the shaking of his head. At intervals he furtively glanced at the chaplain out of the corner of his eye like a criminal peeking at his conscience. He could not escape the feeling of terror, and at the same time of respect, inspired by that strict, relentless investigator of his most hidden inaccessible feelings. He pondered over what the priest had said to him. Each minute was making the truth he had revealed more clear, and what had been obscure was now transparent, just as the light from a star born eons ago finally reaches earth and strikes our mortal eyes.

Once, he interrupted his pacing and raised his eyes to the counselor's portrait. This time he did not withdraw them in terror; he riveted his gaze on the portrait with a look of reproach and bitterness. The priest noted it and smiled sadly. The son's look was calling his father to account. "Peace to the dead!" observed Melchior. "Your father's deeds are no longer under the jurisdiction of this world." Melchior had already got up to leave. "Dr. Camargo," said he, changing his tone, "will be arriving some day soon according to his letter. Is there any reason to delay the wedding?"

"No."

"Do you agree it should take place at once?"

"Yes.'

Melchior walked to the door. He was about to turn the knob but stopped. "Before we part," he said, "I would like a promise from you that you will not speak to Helena before tomorrow."

"I promise."

The priest hesitated a moment; Estacio seemed to read his thought. "You want still another promise?" he asked, "a promise that I will take every means of avoiding her?"

"Yes, that you look upon her as a total stranger."

"Could I do otherwise?" observed Estacio sadly. "What has happened, for the present at least, places a barrier between her and her family. Besides, I would be devoid of all moral sense . . ."

"You swear it?"

"I swear it."

Melchior opened his shirt and disclosed an ivory crucifix hanging at his throat by a black ribbon. "This," he said simply, "is the effigy of your God, an example of chaste purity such as neither the centuries before nor since his coming have seen. Swear to him what you promised me."

"Reverend Father," returned Estacio, "my word was enough. But, if there is need of a more solemn affirmation,

I shall give it as you ask." He inclined his head over the crucifix and kissed it respectfully.

Melchior blessed him.

Leaving the study, they went to the sewing room, where they found Dona Ursula a little less perturbed. "Did you speak to Helena?" she asked the priest.

"Not yet. I know she does not wish to leave her room. Let us allow her to get over the first shock. Tomorrow, I shall come and find out everything. For today it is best for you to try to be calm."

"Oh! I am calm! I have not lost confidence."

Dona Ursula uttered these words with so much serenity and deep conviction that even Melchior's spirits were strengthened, though he was not inclined to believe the worse. The venerable man delayed a few moments, contemplating Dona Ursula's placid countenance, wondering at the secret force that made her deaf to the clamor of reality—at least what appeared to be reality. He silently contemplated her, then went down to the chácara.

## Chapter XXIV

It was dark night. As he trod the earth and gravel of the broad paths through the grounds, he saw in imagination the past bloom again—not always a happy one but generally quiet. More than once he had sought to dissipate the dark shadow that the counselor's infidelities had drawn over his wife's brow. Might there not be in that house a generation of woes destined to beat down wealth's pride with the pitiless spectacle of human frailty?

"No," he said to himself, "everything is connected and evolves logically. As Jesus said, men do not gather figs from thistles. The husband's life of sensuality engendered the wife's intense, concealed unhappiness, and she passed from among us, still in the full bloom of life. The fruit will be as bitter as the tree; it has a flavor laced with remorse." At this point in his thought he arrived at the gate. There he stopped. A cautious, hesitating footstep behind him made him turn his head. A shape, whose face he could not make out in the dark came up beside him and respectfully touched the skirts of his long coat. It was Helena's page.

"Senhor priest," said the boy, "tell me, please, what has happened in the house. I see them all sad. Nhanhan Helena doesn't show her face; shut herself up in her room . . . You pardon slave his boldness? What has happened?"

"Nothing," answered Melchior.

"Oh! It can't be! Something must have happened. Senhor Father doesn't trust his slave. Is Nhanhan Helena sick?"

"Calm down. There is nothing."

"Hmm!" the page ejaculated incredulously. "There is something that slave may not know; but, too, slave may know something that white people would like to hear about . . ."

Melchior repressed an exclamation. The darkness did not allow him to examine the slave's expression, but his voice was sorrowful and sincere. The idea of questioning him passed through the priest's mind but did no more than that. He rejected it at once, as he had rejected it a few hours earlier. Melchior prefered the straight line; he refused to follow a devious path. He would go ask Helena for the solution to the problem. Meanwhile the page, interpreting his silence as encouragement, continued, "Nhanhan Helena is a saint. If anyone blames her they are blaming her for being good. I will tell you all about it . . ."

Melchior was about to refuse, but something occurred to interrupt the page's tale against his will, and perhaps against Melchior's wishes. They heard footsteps; it was another slave who had come to lock the gate. "Someone's coming," said Vicente, "tomorrow . . ."

He groped in the darkness for the priest's hand, found it, kissed it, and hurried away. Melchior went on to his cottage, troubled by the half-revelation he had heard. Another man might have had a moment's doubt of the slave's sincerity, might have supposed his action was less spontaneous than it appeared, in short that Helena herself had thought up this means of waylaying their expectation and winning sympathy for herself. The interpretation was not without verisimilitude, but it had no part in the priest's thoughts. It was to *him* that the apostolic maxim especially applied: *Unto the pure all things are pure.*

The dawn of the next day lighted a sky swept of clouds. Estacio awoke with the light after a restless night. Never did a morning appear more blatantly jolly; never had the air been so finely transparent nor the foliage so lustrous. As he leaned out the window, he saw flowers of every color breaking the green monotony and sending up to him an invisible cloud of aromas—the look of a festival thanks to nature's irony. Estacio found himself in its midst like a funeral procession at carnival time.

He breakfasted alone; Dona Ursula was with Helena. Right after breakfast he received a letter from Mendonça, who had called the day before and been told the same thing as the others; he wrote to learn if there was illness in the house. Estacio sent him a reply in the affirmative, adding that though not serious he would not expect him for a couple of days. This reply might have been more circumspect; in his then state Estacio thought it an excellent one.

Around midday, Melchior arrived. He found Dona Ursula in the drawing room; she had spied him from the window.

"Helena?" he asked anxiously.

"She has already come downstairs; she is more calm. I didn't ask her about anything, but when I told her you were coming to talk with her she seemed anxious to see you, and even asked me to send for you."

They went into the little sitting room adjoining the dining room. Helena sat with her head lying on the back of the chair, and her eyes half closed. As soon as the priest came into the room she opened her eyes and sat up. A deep red momentarily colored her cheeks that were pale from wakefulness and torturing anguish. She rose and took two steps toward the priest, who took her hands in his. "Imprudent girl!" he murmured.

Helena smiled, a wan smile as transitory as the color that had dyed her cheeks. Dona Ursula went to call Estacio. The moment she left, Helena grasped one of the priest's hands. "Will you see him!" she said. "I do not have the courage to speak to anyone but you, to tell you the whole . . ."

"There's no need! I know all about it," Melchior interjected, smiling. "Vicente came to my house this morning. It was his own idea; he told me all he knew, said that the man is your brother, that you were seeing him secretly because you were unable or unwilling to present him in your relatives' house. Your scruples were excessive and your action thoughtless. Why give a wrong appearance to a natural sentiment? You might have spared yourself and your family much distress and many tears if you had, instead, taken the direct way, which is always the better one."

Helena listened to this speech of the priest's with her whole soul starting from her eyes. She did not even appear to breathe. When he finished she asked breathlessly, "What was his purpose in telling you this?"

"The purest imaginable; he was afraid you were in trouble and for that reason came to tell me everything."

Helena joined her hands and raised her eyes. Melchior did not interrupt this mental ascent to heaven; he contented himself with looking at her. Helena's beauty had never seemed to him more touching than in that imploring attitude. "I thanked God," she said lowering her hands, "because he breathed into the vile body of the slave such a noble spirit of devotion. He informed on me in order to restore me to the family's esteem. What no one could have torn out of his heart he tore out himself the moment he saw my name and my peace of mind in danger. Unfortunately he lied."

Melchior turned pale. "He lied without knowing it," she went on. "He told what he thought was the truth, what I had given him as such. That man is not my brother."

Melchior leaned toward her and seizing her hands demanded imperiously: "Then who is he? Your silence accuses you. You no longer have a right to hesitate."

"I do not hesitate. In such situations a creature like me walks straight against a rocky crag or to the edge of an abyss; she is crushed to bits or disappears in the void. There is no room for choice. This letter," she added, drawing a folded paper from her pocket, "will tell you the whole story. Read it and pass on its message to Estacio and Dona Ursula. I don't have the heart to face them now." Melchior, in bewilderment, barely nodded. "When it is read," she continued, "the bonds that attach me to this house will be broken. The blame for what has befallen me is not mine; it lies with others; but I accept the consequences. May I at least count on your blessing?" The priest's answer was to place a kiss on her forehead, a kiss of absolution and clemency, which she repaid with many kisses on his wrinkled hand, a hand that trembled with emotion.

Helena hurried into the hall, leaving the priest alone with the letter in his hand, without daring to open it, fearful of the evils that would rush out of it, without even the certainty that hope would remain at the bottom. He was about to open it but hesitated, doubting whether he should do so in the absence of Estacio and Dona Ursula. He overcame his scruple and read it.

Dona Ursula came back just as he was folding up the letter but drew back in startled amazement. He was white as a ghost. Before either could speak, Estacio came into the room. Melchior went to him and handed him the letter. Estacio unfolded it and read the following:

"My dear daughter, best of daughters, I learned from Vicente that something occurred there to distress you. I think I can guess what it is. Estacio was here just after you left the last time. He came in with a look of mistrust and gave as a reason or pretext the necessity to take care of some cuts on his hand. Perhaps he himself made them in order to get into the house. He asked me questions; I answered as the case required. Suspecting that he had learned of your visits, I did not hide my poverty; it was a means of attributing them to a charitable impulse. Thus virtue served as a cloak for natural instinct. Isn't this in great part the tenor of human life? I was disturbed however; I had probably not removed the thorn from his breast. From what Vicente has told me, I fear such is the case. Tell me what is wrong, my poor beloved daughter. Hide nothing from me. At all events, proceed with caution. Do not provoke a rupture. If necessary, stop coming here for several weeks, or months. I shall be content with the knowledge that you are at peace and living in happy prosperity. I bless you, Helena, with all the affection there is in the heart of the luckiest of fathers, for, though fortune took away everything else, she has not taken from me the pleasure of feeling I am loved by you. Adieu. Write me. Salvador"

"P.S. I have your note. For the love of God, do nothing. Do not leave the family; it would cause a scandal."

Estacio did not immediately comprehend what he had read. The truth seemed to have no verisimilitude. His first impulse was to rush out of the room and go talk to Helena. Melchior stopped him in time. "Let us not be hasty," said he. "First, let us calm down."

Estacio lowered himself into a chair. Melchior communicated the contents of the letter to Dona Ursula, whose stupefaction was even greater than her nephew's. She did not utter a word nor move a muscle; she remained staring stupidly at the paper. There ensued among those three, ten minutes of deathly silence. Dona Ursula was not able to gather her wits; she kept staring at the letter, and then at her nephew and the priest, as if hoping for an answer that her own mind could not discover in the maze of things that had occurred. Estacio was disoriented; he sought in vain for a logical connection between his ideas; the new revelation was one more complication. If the letter was sincere, how explain his father's will? If it was not, how explain the audacity of such a fabrication? He could not discern what was in Helena's favor and did not dare affirm what was against her.

In the middle of that family which was in danger of being broken up, Melchior considered the preference of death to some of life's terrible blows. If an announcement of Helena's death had come, instead of that letter, their grief would be violent, but the finality of the thing and the consolation of religion would have contributed to healing their hearts and converting the despair of a few days into a lifelong memory of happy love. In place of this, he saw perhaps a destiny reduced to nothing and a chasm yawning between hearts that a dead man's will had linked together. Whatever truth there might be in the letter, this would probably be the result.

He left them to go see Helena, to get a more precise explanation of what he had just read. She rose when she saw him and seemed to revive as she observed the benevolent manner in which he spoke to her. A deep sigh of relief broke from her; she let her arms fall on the priest's shoulders, hid her face against his breast, and rested, momentarily, from the sorrow that afflicted her. "Do they forgive me?" she asked.

"They will. Tell me the whole story."

"Oh! I can't, I don't know, I only know he is my father."

The chaplain did not insist. He returned to the other two, whom he found in the same position in which he had left them. They questioned him with their eyes.

"Nothing!" he replied. "She is in no state of mind to answer our questions now. Besides, she probably does not know the whole story. We have the first admission of the truth . . ."

"Of the truth?" interrupted Estacio gloomily. "Who knows whether what we read on that paper is the truth?"

"It is, it has to be. We lack, to be sure, the bases of his asseveration but I shall take it upon myself to go discover them."

"We will both go."

Dona Ursula was decided in her effort to dissuade her nephew from going to the house of the fellow who was the cause of their family troubles, not so much because she thought it improper for there to be any relations between Estacio and him, as because she needed someone to be with her in these grave circumstances. Melchior inclined to Dona Ursula's opinion. "I will go alone," said he. "Later I will bring him here if need be."

"I cannot wait," insisted Estacio, "I must speak to that man, hear him, read truth or falsehood in the lines of his face. Perhaps family dignity demands something else; but, Reverend Father, my heart is bleeding . . ."

It was impossible to dissuade him. Melchior undertook only to moderate his impetuosity. As for that, it *was* a violent situation, and critical; it behooved them to resolve it without delay and without hesitation. The priest told Dona Ursula to be of good cheer and left accompanied by Estacio, whose heart, now that it had recovered from the first shock, was abandoning the regions of doubt to enter the atmosphere of truth, at least of hope. Whatever might be the consequences of the new revelation, it came as balm after his painful agitation; it was a shred of blue rent in the stormy sky of those days. This is what he was thinking—or, rather, feeling, for thought did not venture to govern him while his whole existence was centered in his heart.

Arrived at the cottage, Estacio turned away his eyes; it was hard for him to even look at it, but he got the better of himself. There was some delay in answering their knock; finally the door opened and the figure of the master of the house appeared. On seeing them he paled a little but attempted to hide the impression with a smile. Estacio came straight to the point.

"I imagine you remember me?" he said.

"Perfectly."

"Do you know what brings us here?"

"No, sir."

"Do you admit you wrote this letter?"

Salvador started, then made a gesture in the affirmative.

"Do you claim that Helena is your daughter?" Estacio asked after a moment. "Will you confirm verbally what you wrote?"

"Helena is my daughter."

Melchior intervened: "My old friend Counselor Valle, who died a year ago, acknowledged Helena as his daughter by a clause in his will; he recommended that his family treat her with affection and tenderness; and he named the boarding school in which she was then being educated. The act of recognition and the circumstances mentioned give complete veracity to the word of the deceased. What proof, sir, can you offer in opposition to it?"

"None," said Salvador, "I do not have proof of any sort."

"In the absence of proof," pursued the chaplain, "could you tell us how you can suppose a falsification on the part of the counselor when treating of such a serious disposition as this of introducing a strange young woman into his family?"

Salvador smiled bitterly. "Suppose," said he, "that I betrayed his confidence and that he believed he was Helena's father."

"Was it that?"

"No, it was not. In the situation in which we now find ourselves, there is no longer room for half-truths. Perforce all must be told. Let me have ten minutes; it will suffice."

All three sat down. Melchior stared at the man with the persistent curiosity natural to the occasion. Salvador remained silent for several moments. Finally he turned to the chaplain. "I am grateful," he said, "that your reverence has seen fit to come; your charity will temper the righteous indignation of this young man, and I will be able to make the indispensable declarations in the presence of the two persons whom I most love after Helena."

"Please begin," Estacio said coldly.

## Chapter XXV

"Helena's mother," said Salvador, "whose beauty was the cause both of her misfortune and of her good fortune, was the daughter of an aristocratic planter of Rio Grande do Sul, where I too was born. We fell in love with each other. My father opposed our marriage; he was a man of some means, had sent me to school, and wanted to see me in high public office. Angela, he said, would be an obstacle to my career. He opposed; I resisted. I seduced her and ran away with her. We went to live in eastern territory, then we went on to Montevideo and later to Rio de Janeiro. I was twenty years old when I left my father's house. I possessed some little education, a few milreis, much love, and great hope. It was more than enough for my time of life but not enough for a future. The honeymoon was soon a dark night of privations and hard work. My life became a mosaic of trades and professions. I have been a peddler, rent collector, bookkeeper, farmer, factory hand, inn-keeper, registry clerk; for a few weeks I made my living making copies of plays and actors' parts. I worked hard but fortune did not match my diligence, and I wasted my best years in a harsh, unequal struggle. There was one compen-sation, the sweetest possible; it was Angela's love and cheer-fulness, the equanimity with which she faced all our vicissi-tudes. A short time after our elopement there was an addi-tional compensation, Helena. That little girl was born in one of the sorriest periods of my life. Broths for the young mother were furnished by a neighbor woman. But the child was born at a lucky moment and was another tie that held us together. The presence of a new being, blood of my blood, made me redouble my efforts. I worked with my whole soul, struggled resolutely against adverse forces, secure in the thought of finding at night the mother's solic-itude and the daughter's eager caresses. You gentlemen are not fathers; you cannot appreciate the power of a daugh-ter's smile to dissipate all the sad worries accumulated on a man's brow. Many a time when I had worked into the night, and though of a robust constitution came home exhausted, I would go to Helena's cradle, gaze at her a moment and seem to gather new strength. Her very cradle was the work of my hands! I fashioned it out of some old pine boards, a crude, but sublime, piece of work: it served to lull to sleep one half of my paradise on earth."

Salvador broke off overcome by emotion. "Forgive me," he said after a few moments, "if these memories touch my heart. I was poor, as poor as today. From that time there remains only a sad, consoling echo. As Helena grew, her graces increased. She was the enchanted magic and hope of my poor home. When she was old enough to learn her letters it was I who gave her her first lessons. In amazement I assisted at the dawn of that intelligence which you gentlemen have seen today so well developed and lucid. She learned with facility because she loved to study. Angela and I built the most handsome air castles in the world. We saw her already a woman, beautiful — as she actually came to be — because she was already beautiful, intelligent and gifted, the wife of some man who would adore her and raise her in the world. We lived on this expectation, though it was only a dream, and did not feel the blows dealt us by fortune."

"Why, sir," asked Melchior, "given your love and the daughter born to you, did you not sanctify your condition?"

"The question is just," replied Salvador, "but the answer is plain. Marriage would be our justification; it would be an argument against my father's resentment. In the first days of our flight from Rio Grande, the intoxication of our felicity did away with all idea of sanctifying and legalizing a union consented to by nature. Then came the hardship and poverty. As I was in myself certain that I would not abandon the responsibilities I had taken upon my shoulders, I kept putting off the act from month to month, from year to year. Finally the idea was completely forgotten. We were bound together by our poverty and by our hearts, we did not aspire to society's respect; a sad excuse and the recollection still more sad, because our marriage would perhaps have forestalled the occurrences that followed. Helena was six years old. My fortunes adverse up to then, with rare intervals of good luck, seemed to be improving a little. I was about to enter a new phase of life, when a grave situation called me to Rio Grande. My father had fallen ill; he sent me his pardon, bidding me come to him without delay. I promptly obeyed. I left part of the sum he had sent for traveling expense with Angela and Helena, and set out. Twenty-four hours after seeing my father, I suffered the grief of losing him. The liquidation of his business took little time; his wealth all went to his creditors; I was left with a few milreis. I received this new blow with the philosophy of insensibility. Who knows if I was not the one to blame for what had happened. These affairs, though conducted with dispatch, kept me there longer than I had intended and had agreed upon. My anxiety to return increased when I did not receive any answer to the last letters I had written Angela. Finally I succeeded in returning to Rio Janeiro with one more sorrow and one less hope. At this point your father enters the drama."

Estacio turned away his eyes.

"As soon as I arrived, I hurried to our house and found it shut up. A neighbor, noting my anxiety, informed me that Angela had moved to São Christovão. He did not know the number of the house, nor the name of the street but he gave me directions by which to find it. I still have before my eyes the smile with which he gave these answers. It was a pitying smile that humiliated. Although he had never received the slightest offense from me, I am sure he took a secret pleasure in my misfortune. Why? I leave it to the philosophers to solve this puzzle of human nature. I spent a lot of time looking for the house but finally found it. When I saw it I couldn't believe my eyes and thought the man's directions were wrong. It was an elegant house hidden among trees and in the middle of a little garden. Could that be the residence of the companion of my poverty? From a feeling of dread, I hesitated to go knock at the door; then I saw a man come to the gate, whom I took to be the gardener. I asked for the lady of the house by her own name, saying that I wished to speak to her. "My mistress is not at home," he answered abstractedly. I told him I would wait, but the gardener said he was going to leave and had to lock the gate, that his mistress would not be home till night. 'I will wait,' I retorted. The gardener measured me from head to foot, looked cautiously up and down the street, and then said in a low tone, 'I advise you, sir, not to come back. The boss won't like it.' I am not writing a novel; I will dispense with portraying the effect his words produced on me. What I felt exceeds all description. There are more solemn catastrophes, there are more pathetic situations, but at that moment I felt that all the sorrows of the world had converged on my breast. The gardener was genuinely kindhearted. Reading the effect of his words in my face, he said something to me of which I have absolutely no recollection. He gently urged me to leave. I obeyed mechanically. Though I could have found out about Angela right then I failed to do so. A fever kept me in bed for three days, a poor bed in the worst inn in Cidade Nova. On the third day, I received a letter from Angela, begging me to forgive her for the step she had taken, saying she had been led by a new mad passion and if she should come to regret it, that would be my revenge. When I read her letter, I had a desire to go and strangle her, but it passed, and my grief dissolved away in reflections. A few days before, on board ship, an English engineer on his way from Rio Grande to this city had lent me a dog-eared volume of Shakespeare. I had little left of the little English I'd learned at school but I deciphered, word by word, as best I could; and one speech I came upon sent a chill through me as if it were a prophecy. I recalled it later when Angela wrote me. 'She has deceiv'd her father,' Brabantio said to Othello, 'and may do thee.' It was good reasoning, at least it was understandable. Two days after Angela's letter, I wrote her asking for a half hour's conversation, nothing more. Angela granted me the interview. My intention was to steal Helena. It would seem Angela had foreseen it, for she received me alone, in the garden at nine o'clock in the evening."

"Why do you recall all these minutiae?" Melchior interposed gently. "All we wish is to learn the essentials."

"Everything in my narrative is essential," said Salvador. "The interview completely enlightened me as to Angela's character. What other woman would risk braving the anger of a spurned man in such circumstances? Angela was a complex of singular qualities. Capable of enduring the greatest trials, brave and cheerful in the midst of extreme privation, she forgot in an instant the virtues she possessed to run after a will-o'-the-wisp love affair. It was not wealth that seduced her; she would have gone even if she had to exchange wealth for poverty. Angela was by nature half nun and half ballerina; capable of enduring the austerities of the cloister, she was no less eager for the theater's tawdry display. But what of that . . . wasn't I the one who led her from the king's highway into an obscure bypath? That night I tried to be calm and superior to what had occurred. 'I have but one aim,' I told her, 'to take Helena away with me. She is my daughter, I do not want her left to the influence of your bad example.' The tears with which she bathed my hands, her entreaties as she knelt at my feet that I would leave Helena with her — there was no denying it was all sincere. I yielded in appearance but my resolve was fixed. Without Helena life appeared impossible. What other tie bound me to this world? Death and poverty had made a desolate waste around me. The only happiness remaining was she."

"Second abduction," observed the priest. "You were about to condemn yourself to obtaining a mere glimmer of happiness through violent means."

"You are right," Salvador replied sadly; "one hell evokes another hell. Happy are those who follow the straight path and never pull away from it. I decided to steal Helena. I watched night and day but never once saw her. The house seldom had a door or even a window open; it was all secrecy and mystery. One day I resolved to go see Angela's protector. People had told me that Counselor Valle was the most honorable man in the world. I was convinced he would hear me and yield to my just petition. The devil of a pride prevented the execution of this plan of mine. About to enter the counselor's house, I drew back.

Two or three months went by. I grew thin, long sleepless
nights had made me pale, work held no attraction for me,
I began to suffer from hunger. The poet who said that
longing is a delightful pricking sensation in the breast did
not consult my heart. I found it bitter sharp; it is true it
was mixed with anger, the anger of the powerless, and the
deadly resentment of the abandoned. One day I went to
São Christovão, ready to use force to take Helena away
with me, or to march straight to the Aljube prison. It was
late afternoon. As I drew near the garden, I heard my
daughter's voice. It was the first time in many long months!
My heart stopped beating. After the first start of emotion,
I moved cautiously along the hedge; Helena was talking to
someone. Through an opening in the hedge, I could see
her. She was on a man's lap. That man was the counselor.
I looked from one to the other, now at my rival, now at
Helena. Helena was caressing his beard; he was smiling at
her with such an air of tenderness as to almost absolve him
from his offense against me. At the same time, my chest
tightened as I saw her give another man caresses to which
only I had a right. It was a theft against nature. But if my
own heart rejected me what could I exact from other
hearts? After a time — I don't know whether after a long or
a short time because I had been staring vacantly at them
both, stupefied by love and anger — I heard them talking
about me. 'Tell me,' Helena was saying, 'when is papa
coming?' The counselor gave her a kiss and spoke of a butterfly that had lighted on her head. Children, however, are
implacable; she repeated her question. 'Papa is not coming
back,' the counselor answered. Helena was troubled: 'Not
coming back? Why not?' 'Your mama said yesterday that
papa is in heaven.' Helena put her hands to her eyes and
wept. A cloud passed over my eyes. I tried to take a few
steps, to enter the garden, to say who I was and demand
my daughter. My muscles did not respond to my intention;
my knees buckled and I fell. When I came to, I again

looked toward the place where I had seen them. They were still there but the picture was different. The counselor had got up, holding Helena in his arms, and she was no longer crying. He was kissing her little hands and saying, 'If papa went to heaven I am still here in his place to give you many kisses, many sweets, and many dolls. Do you want to be my daughter?' Helena's response was that of a shipwrecked soul; she put her arms around his neck as if to say, 'I have no one else in the world!' The gesture was so eloquent that I saw tears well up in the counselor's eyes. Those tears decided my fate. I saw that he loved her, and of all the sacrifices the human heart can make I made the greatest, the most painful; I did away with my paternity, I gave up the only heritage that I had on earth, the strength of my youth, consolation in my poverty, the crown of my old age, and I returned to my desolate solitude more brokenhearted than ever!" Salvador interrupted his narration, raised his right hand to his eyes; between his fingers there flowed some tears, which he quickly wiped away in embarrassment.

"These recollections are painful for you," said the priest. "It is best not to evoke them, ever; it means opening wounds that time has healed. We now know the essential facts . . ."

"No, there is still something more," said Salvador.

Estacio had got up. Visibly moved, he tried to struggle against the feelings that overpowered him, in order to maintain the necessary independence of mind to pass judgment on the narrative and on the extent of its importance. He had involuntarily shaken Salvador's hand on hearing his last words, then repented the impulsive gesture as if it might appear to be a summary absolution. The truth is he was not thinking or feeling clearly; his mind and heart were a battlefield for contrary ideas and emotions.

"I have come to the end of my story," said Salvador after a few minutes. "All that remains is to explain Helena's actions."

## *Chapter XXVI*

"Your father," continued Salvador, addressing Estacio, who had gone to the window to regain his composure and now sat down again, "your father was honorable and gentlemanly. In taking Angela from me he did not betray me, because he had never seen me; he did not contribute directly to her betrayal, because he supposed our relations had been cut. I learned later that when he and Angela fell in love, she hid from him the purpose of my trip. She led him to believe she was separated from me. She lied, as she lied later in saying I had died. The counselor did not even know my name. Her lie in the first instance was without motive, there was no calculation, it was prompted by love or a slip of memory; it was perhaps a way of showing me respect; in the second instance there was calculation: it was intended to redouble the counselor's affection for Helena. And that was the result; he came to feel he was Helena's father, and he assumed the character from that very afternoon. As for the contract made between the man and the child, he carried out all its terms with punctual generosity. As you may easily believe, I was deeply grateful to him. Once, passing a print shop, I saw his portrait; I bought it and keep it there beside Helena's."

Melchior and Estacio glanced at the wall where there hung two pictures, still covered as Estacio had seen them the first day he went there.

"The months and the years passed," continued Salvador, "Helena was entered in a boarding school in Botafogo, where she received a select education. The counselor enrolled her there, representing her as the orphan of a friend from Minas. Angela, who passed as her aunt, would bring her home on Saturdays. I shall omit a thousand intermediate circumstances, and the few times I succeeded in seeing my daughter from a hidden spot as she passed by. If time had produced in me its usual effects, if nature had not compensated for fortune by preserving my vigor and the freshness of youth, perhaps I might have found a means of getting a job at Helena's school or in its neighborhood in order to see her more frequently. But I had not changed. When the initial shock had passed, my flesh returned, my color also, and I was the same as I had been before going to Rio Grande. Helena might recognize me and I would be breaking the unspoken agreement I had made with the counselor. One Saturday, however, when Helena was twelve, she and her mother coming from the school stopped the carriage in front of the Passeio Publico. I saw them get out and enter the park. Led by an irresistible impulse, I too went in. I wanted to look at her from a distance, without speaking to them, but the resolve was beyond my strength. What father would not have done as I did? In the most secluded part of the Passeio, I ran up to Helena. When she saw me the little girl appeared not to recognize me immediately, but considered me closely a few moments, then drew back in terror and clung to her mother, her arms around her mother's waist. I understood that it was not a father before her but a spectre returned from the other world. I was about to move away when I heard Helena asking her mother, 'Papa?' I turned. Angela had hidden the child's face in her garments. The gesture amounted to a confession; but it was still more plainly so when the mother, yielding to her better nature, resolutely straightened her shoulders, uncovered her daughter's face, placed a kiss on her forehead, looked into her eyes, and made an affirmative gesture with her head. The little girl did not wait for more; she ran to me and threw herself into my arms. Angela did not try to prevent her daughter's action; the past and my sacrifices spoke in my favor. I embraced Helena and kissed her like a man gone mad. Angela intervened. 'Enough!' she said. She grasped her daughter's hand and held out her own to me. I took it mechanically. My eyes were fastened on the child. She was so lovely in her costly dress, her hair tied with blue ribbons and with a charming little straw hat, and her tiny feet encased in satin boots! 'You did right,' I said to Angela after a few moments, 'you gave her a better father than I.' I noticed then that she herself had been transformed; she was elegantly dressed and was superlatively handsome. Wealth had improved on nature. I gazed at her without envy, without resentment, but with nostalgia, this time pleasurable because I called to mind the happy days of our intoxication and madness. The past is a private hoard of savings for those who no longer expect anything from the present or from the future; it contains living sensations that bridge time's gaps. 'I did wrong,' she said to me in a low voice. She sighed. 'I know that I am dead,' I told her, 'and I have no intention of coming back to life.' I turned to Helena; 'My daughter, remember, you have not seen me. I died as far as you know and as far as the world cares. Your father is another man. Promise me that you will say nothing.' Helena nodded slightly, and furtively kissed my hand as if she did not want to be seen by Angela. From that simple gesture I knew that she would follow my instruction; but her look of sadness was punishment to her mother. We were asking of nature more than it could give."

Salvador paused, got up and went to the chest of drawers, took a little box from one of the drawers and placed it on the table. Melchior and Estacio exchanged a look of curiosity. Salvador sat down again.

"Angela died," he continued, "a year later. Your father and a handful of friends went to the burial. I too was present. The difference was that he was burying an amorous adventure; I saw my whole past interred. I saw him sad and taciturn, as one sincerely mourning the woman he had lost. As for Helena, since she could not remain alone in the house, she was placed in the school as a permanent boarder. The counselor visited her every week. As for me, relying on my daughter's discretion, I entered into a correspondence with her; it was all the consolation I could have. A slave girl at the school served as our intermediary. Then as now I found a compassionate soul ready to help me to happiness with her secrecy. The difference is that at that time a pecuniary intervention was required. I had little, but I would give up the day's dinner in order to read a letter from Helena. I have kept them all, those from long ago and the ones from the last few months; they are locked up here." He pointed to the box he had placed on the table.

"One day, when I was having a late breakfast in a tavern, I read the notice of the counselor's death. It filled me with consternation but if, by your leave, the whole truth be told, I felt a kind of satisfaction mixed with my grief. At last I could breathe freely! Our contract had expired with him; I was going to enter into the possession of my daughter. I did not write to Helena right away; I did so after a few days. I had two replies: the first had the same feeling as my letter; the second informed me that the counselor had recognized her in his will. I could look for the second letter and read it to you; it is a proof of the elevated sentiments of that child. She expressed herself with the greatest gratitude and love in respect to the counselor; but she refused to accept the posthumous favor. Knowing the truth, she was unwilling to hide it from the world. By accepting the recognition, she considered that she would be prejudicing the rights of the other heirs, in addition to formally repudiating me, something she was unwilling to do now that she had acquired freedom of action. 'Between the inheritance and duty,' she said, 'I choose what is honorable, just, and natural.' This letter took away my sleep an entire night, perplexed as I was over the late counselor's act and his heir's decision. What invisible hand had touched the chord of sensibility in the counselor's heart? Much better to have translated his affection for Helena into a simple bequest. I reflected about this for a long time: father struggled with father. To have her with me was my future, my dream, my ambition; it was a reality that I had succeeded in touching with my hands. But could I tie her to my fortune's decrepit chariot? give her a bitter daily bread? The counselor's family would assure her a future, respect, prestige; the law would support her. I asked myself whether, after having died to the world, I was free to come back to life and lay claim to a title that I had stripped myself of; in short if I now possessed the right to cause a scandal? If these reflections had come alone they would have triumphed immediately, but in opposition to them came suggestions from the heart. I took note of the fact that in yielding to the will of the dead man I would be cutting a chasm between myself and Helena and that I could no longer, or only rarely and in secret, enjoy the felicity of telling her I loved her and of hearing a like response from her heart. I spent three whole days in this conflict. Helena wrote me another letter insisting on the resolution she said she had taken, urging me to answer her. I did, sacrificing myself. I did not convince her. I tried to get to see her. It was not easy, but interest overcame all obstacles: the slave who was our intermediary raised the price of her accommodation. What passed between Helena and me I cannot repeat here. The time allowed for our appointment was short but our conflict was hotly debated and intense. I sought to persuade her with arguments and entreaties; she resisted with indignation and tears. Her noble nature scorned complicity and the wealth to be gained from a usurpation. I saw no usurpation because in my eyes neither the interests of the counselor's family nor notions of simple morality prevailed; I saw my daughter and her future, nothing more. Perhaps those to blame for my way of thinking were Angela and her benefactor. They had accustomed me to love Helena from a distance and not take offense at the benefits she received at the hands of another. Finally, my egotistical, lacerated heart considered that the recognition of the poor child was a simple return for the caresses I had been cheated of.

That is the way my conscience reasoned. Helena resisted to the very last; she yielded only to a necessity to obey, to the image of her mother, which I invoked as a supreme effort, to my assurance that I would always be with her, that I would go live near her wherever fate took her. She yielded from exhaustion, yielded without conviction or fervor. If there is any blame attached to Helena's final course of action, it is all mine because I was its sole author; she was nothing more than the instrument, a rebellious yet passive instrument. Her mistake was not to have the necessary prudence to refuse to leap across the chasm that separated us. I ought to have reckoned with her quick decisions and promptly executed plans—there she resembled her mother. Though I sent her word, with precise details of where I lived, I was far from expecting her to come to see me. At first I was terrified at the possible consequences; but if a man can accustom himself to bad luck and sorrow why can't he accustom himself to pleasure and prosperity? Helena came again and then again. The joy of seeing her made me forget the danger and in those rare, furtive hours I drank deep the only happiness that remained for me on earth, that of being a father and of feeling myself loved by my daughter."

## Chapter XXVII

He had finished. Tears that he had kept back with difficulty welled in his eyes and rolled down his cheeks. He was not alone in his emotional outburst; his two hearers also were moved. He had finished, and it was the worst thing that could happen. Once his narration was ended, the other two remained silent and perplexed, yet did not venture to question its truth.

After a short pause, Salvador added this conclusion: "I have no other proof of what I have told you except these letters, which are probably proof enough, and my tears which will be eternal. But even if there were other proof I do not believe it is necessary. For the situation we are in there are only two possible solutions: either nothing is changed, all remains as the counselor willed, and I alone assume the unlucky consequences by disappearing, or the family rejects Helena and I take her away with me. You may say the law protects her at all hazards. Then she will sign the necessary releases . . ."

Estacio cut short his speech saying they would give him an answer in due time. He and Melchior left not long after. They walked along without exchanging a single word, each absorbed in his own thoughts. The priest, however, kept glancing at Estacio from time to time, trying to divine his thoughts. Arrived at the chácara gate, he said to him, "What do you intend to do?"

"I don't yet know."

"I know what you ought to do — nothing."

"Keep things as they are?"

"Yes. Helena obeyed the will of her two fathers, accepting the false situation in which they both contrived to place her. She obeyed perforce. Now, she has been recognized; it is a fact we cannot controvert or alter."

Estacio remained silent a few moments.

"But can I, in view of what we have just heard, can I let Helena keep a title that actually does not belong to her? Helena is not my sister, she is absolutely unrelated to our family, the title that connected her with us has disappeared. What reason is there for us to perpetuate a lie . . ."

"Of your father's?" interjected Melchior.

"Reverend Father!"

"That man spoke the truth, but neither the law nor the Church is satisfied with your simple truth. In opposition to it there is the final declaration of a dead man. Civil law demands more than words and tears; ecclesiastic law does not delete with a stroke of the pen a posthumous affirmation. Furthermore, do not imagine that this man will appear before anyone and make the assertions he has just made to us, he will only do so when he has lost all hope. It is evident he wishes to alter nothing of the arrangement made by your father and would sooner sacrifice himself than bring shame on his daughter. Are you disposed to do what he refuses to do?

Estacio made no reply. They had entered the chácara and were walking slowly toward the house. Melchior detained him. "Estacio!" he said after looking at him a moment. "I understand, you would like to strip Helena of the title your father bequeathed her and give her another title, attach her to your family by a different tie . . ."

Estacio made a gesture of protest.

"You are forgetting two important things, the scandal and the marriage of one and the other. You no longer belong to yourself, nor does she belong to herself. Come! Be a man. Let us bury all that has taken place in the deepest silence, and yesterday's situation will be the same as tomorrow's."

When they went inside they found that Dona Ursula knew the whole story; she had succeeded in loosening Helena's tongue. Overcome by the reading of the letter, Dona Ursula's spirits were not raised by the girl's verbal narration. Perhaps she would have preferred that Helena actually be the counselor's daughter. The space of a few months and their affectionate life together had produced the difference in feeling between the first and the last day.

"We can do nothing right away," said the priest. "We would provoke a scandal to no purpose."

Dona Ursula made a gesture of assent. Summoned to hear them, Helena came down in a few minutes. Her face colored with shame as soon as she saw Estacio, who was waiting for her at Melchior's side. Neither man spoke but they showed no trace of disapproval. After a long oppressive silence, Estacio informed Helena of the family's decision and expressed their feelings of generosity and confidence. He concluded by saying that his father's last wish would prevail over everything else. Helena turned white and closed her eyes. Dona Ursula ran to her side. The body, weakened by the wakefulness and agitation of these last hours, could no longer hold up. The loss of consciousness was brief. Coming to herself, she fervently kissed Dona Ursula's hands, and the priest's, and extended her own hand to Estacio, who took it in his. Then she said in broken tones, "My heart will be eternally grateful for the remnant of esteem that I have not lost. The situation has changed and one must change with it. I do not ask the protection of the law nor can I accept the indulgence of your friendly hearts. I erred and I must pay for it. As long as only I knew my shame, it was possible to continue living in this house; I muffled my conscience to forget it; but now that it is known I will see it in everyone's eyes and in everyone's smile. I beg you to forgive me and let me go away! I should never have entered this house, that is certain. I am expiating the weakness of a heart I had become accustomed to love from a distance with the fascination of mystery and the enchantment of forbidden fruit. From now on I will love *you* from a distance or from near by, but as an outsider . . . and forgiven!"

When she finished, Helena embraced Dona Ursula as if pleading for the help of her intercession. Dona Ursula returned the embrace but gently shook her head in a gesture of refusal. Melchior observed that Helena's opposition was a sign of detachment not easily understood in relation to the family that, in spite of recent events, had not withdrawn its esteem or its protection.

"She has inherited her father's pride!" murmured Estacio.

The words were spoken in a low tone, but Helena heard,

and her eyes shone with a momentary satisfaction. To attribute to pride what was shame and remorse gave her a certain superiority she thought she lacked in this time of crisis. She protested in the name of her feelings of gratitude with the quick, spirited, warm style of speaking all three knew so well, only interrupted at intervals by her inner agitation and by the tears that streamed from eyes exhausted from crying.

Estacio put an end to her perplexities. "Well," said he, "that is for later. We will obey the law, and our wish is that you obey us."

Helena bit her lip in desperation but made no reply. Her head gradually drooped as if with the weight of an idea that became more and more oppressive. Then she raised her head; her eyes, sad but animated by the last rays of her hope, turned to Estacio's, which at that moment spoke all the pain and grief of his smothered, rebellious passion. They both lowered their glance, fearful of themselves.

"I do not believe she will easily accept your decision," Melchior said to Estacio as soon as he could speak to him alone. "Take precautions, she is capable of running away."

"You think so?"

"Do you not yet know her? The position these events have placed her in is more repugnant to her than anything else. She prefers poverty to shame, and the idea that you privately do not absolve her is the worm that gnaws at her heart."

That night Estacio received a letter from Salvador accompanied by a package. "I have reflected deeply during these two hours," he wrote, "and I have arrived at one conclusion: I eliminate myself. It is the way to preserve Helena's respectability and future, things I cannot give her. When this letter reaches you, I shall have disappeared forever. Do not try to find me; it will be useless. I will bless you from afar. Let all your resentment fall on me; I only deserve it because I was the one that provoked it. Herewith go Helena's letters; I am keeping only three of them as a remembrance of the happiness I have lost."

Estacio was taken with a desire to read Helena's letters, but drew back in time, and ordered them to be given to her. She was with Dona Ursula and handed them to her. "They are my history," said she. "I beg you to read them and judge me." There was a strange, unusual expression in her eyes. She immediately retired to her room, where she lay motionless a long time without uttering a sound, ominously still, her body cast down on a sofa, her soul God knows in what regions of infinite despair.

## Chapter XXVIII

It was on the second night of those extraordinary occurrences that Estacio felt all the violence of the love Helena had inspired in him. As long as they were held in check by a sacred bond, he had loved her without knowing it; and even after he was enlightened by the priest, the efforts expended in mastering himself, and the very nature of the catastrophe did not permit him to see the extent of his ill fortune. Now, yes, the bonds broken, truth restored, he recognized nature's voice, more sincere and stronger than society's arrangements, calling them, one to the other, and that the woman destined to love him and be loved by him was the very woman society's laws forbade him to possess.

During the first hours, his rebellious heart champed at necessity's tight rein. His struggle in the night was intense and cruel, but finally reflection calmed the inner storm, or, rather, shone a light on the wreckage. He saw that the priest was right, that it was imperative to strip away that transitory hope of his. At the same time, Helena's example gave him courage. Mistress of the secret of her birth, and conscious of loving without crime, she had nevertheless hastened his marriage and had chosen for herself a husband for whom she felt nothing more than respect. If a telltale word once broke from her lips, she soon retracted it, making the most obscure of sacrifices.

Estacio refused to be less generous. Early the next morning he wrote Mendonça, asking him to visit them that day without fail. He did not do it without pain, but he did it without regrets. His aim was to hasten Helena's marriage and his own, condemning himself to suffer in silence the blows of an unkind fortune.

Morning, meanwhile, did not bring Helena forgetfulness and peace. Night had not served as a remedy, rather, it bequeathed to the dawn all its mortal anguish. Weakened, nervous, impatient, Helena could not regain her composure, nor even bear up. Now she would coldly repel Dona Ursula's kind words, now ask her to intercede with Estacio in favor of the only solution she recognized as sparing her shame. Her spiritual agitation was great; she tried to quiet it with persuasion. She avoided everyone. She could not face Estacio and Dona Ursula without blushing with shame, an effect all the more visible inasmuch as sleepless nights and grieving had made her very pale. They kept telling her that the counselor's wish constituted a law in the family, according to which she continued to be a relative as before, and as loved as always. She thanked them for their generosity but she could not escape the idea that she had been part of a usurpation. She wanted them to let her go to her father, with whom nature and her conscience told her she could stay without remorse. Estacio and Dona Ursula responded with loving words and objections; but when they saw that these were without effect there was nothing left but to inform her of Salvador's letter.

Father Melchior undertook to make this delicate communication. "Your father," said he, "performed a heroic act for your sake: he went away that he might not make you lose the consideration in which you are held, and your hopes for the future. Read this letter and see if it will give you strength to bear up."

Helena greedily reached for the letter, read it at a glance. The heartfelt groan that broke from her showed the depth of the wound she had received. The priest gathered her in his arms, faint and weeping; spoke words of comfort and hope. In the first moments she did not hear anything; the blow had deafened all feeling. Melchior made her sit down beside him; she obeyed without knowing what she did. After several minutes of silent concentration, she spoke to the priest, thanking him for his kindness. Then she related the events of her childhood (which he had already heard). Her natural quickness of intellect had soon made her see that her mother's position was not like that of other mothers. This discovery, however, had no other effect than to give the daughter's love an intensity and energy capable of facing down the greatest obstacles, as if she wished to unite in herself the whole gamut of love and respect that society guarantees to regular family situations. Melchior heard her with emotion; nourished by the Gospel's pabulum, he recognized an effect of divine grace in that immaculate love, which was worth all the absolutions on earth. He praised and comforted her; he spoke to her of the future, of her family's tender concern — *her* family in spite of everything, finally of her obligation to return their confidence.

Perhaps Helena, in her reasoning mind, agreed with Melchior's counsel; but reason was what governed her least in those troubled circumstances. She left the priest and retired to her apartment. When Dona Ursula went there a half hour later, she found her profoundly depressed; the violence of the crisis had passed. The language in which Dona Ursula spoke to her was maternal and anointed with love and forgiveness. Helena listened to her with gratitude, but a faint, incredulous smile half parted her lips. She imagined she read pity where there was affection and respect, and her pride rebelled at inspiring the only sentiment that her conscience told her she deserved.

Dona Ursula's entreaties that she take nourishment were unavailing. She would eat only enough to ward off starvation. Company was abhorrent to her, and few visitors saw her during the days following that terrible morning, Mendonça no more than the others. The family were careful to announce that Helena was not feeling well. Her intended husband's distress was great, but they all tried to reassure him. Since no word of what had happened had got out, it was easy to sustain their explanation.

Melchior strongly recommended that the family watch her carefully. He feared that with her bold, tenacious spirit she would either run away from home or have recourse to some other act of desperation. He diligently tried to arouse a feeling of resignation in her. The religious character of his authority, the spiritual influence he held over her, were powerful weapons tempered by the sincere paternal love that bound him to her. He spared nothing, but his efforts bore no more fruit than the family's. Helena could not tolerate her situation.

Once, when she had gone down to the chácara, Estacio went in search of her and found her only at the end of some minutes. He found her beside the cistern, where he had spoken with her a few days before, seated on the same wooden bench. She trembled at the sight of him. He came to her, relieved to have finally found her. It was a gray day; huge black clouds hung in the air, swollen with an approaching storm. Estacio urged her to go inside.

"Let me stay here a bit longer," she answered.

"No more than a couple of minutes."

He sat down beside her; they remained silent. Helena had a stick in her hand; Estacio started to take it from her but she threw it to a distance. He got up and went after it.

Only then did he see that one end was wet to a certain point; he decided it might be the depth of water in the cistern. The cistern was shallow, it could not cause death but the suspicion that Helena would not shrink from suicide naturally frightened him. Thinking that the cause did not warrant such an act, he asked himself whether the events of those days might not have clouded the girl's reason. He sat down again and spoke to her with gentleness.

As she listened to his voice, Helena felt a kind of resurrection of other hours that had forever slipped away, a smile enlivened her colorless lips, while her sad, dulled eyes appeared to revive with a remnant of light. Estacio spoke to her of herself, of their approaching marriages, of future happiness. Then he insisted that she go in. A strong wind was commencing to sway the trees, and the storm threatened to break any moment.

"Not yet," she said, "a few minutes more."

"But it can make you ill . . ."

"Perhaps, if everyone wishes for my good health. There are those so cursed by fortune that the very persons who try to make them happy only succeed in making their misfortune. That was my fate. Your father and my mother had no other intention. My own father was led by the same impulse when he obliged me to be an accomplice in his generous lie. Even now that he abandons me with the sole purpose of not taking away my happiness, he has wrested from me the last resource in which I had placed my hope . . ."

"Helena!" interrupted Estacio.

"The last," she repeated.

Her smile had vanished, her eyes were opaque. Estacio was struck with fear at her look of dull concentration; he grasped her arm. She trembled and looked at him.

At first it was a simple meeting of the eyes, but within a few seconds it was something more. It was the first revelation, tacit but conscious, of the feeling that bound them together. Neither of them had sought this coming together of souls but neither shrank from it. What they said with their eyes alone cannot be written on paper, cannot be repeated for human ears—a secret, mysterious confession made from one heart to the other, heard only in heaven because it was not said in the language of earth, nor did they speak for this earth. Their hands of themselves joined, as their glances had; no shame, no fear, no consideration held back that fusion of two beings born to form a single existence.

The wind suddenly blew strong; a rude gust awoke them at an unlucky moment because there are dreams that are meant to end in the reality of the next world. Estacio stood up, bravely shook off felicity's benumbing daze, and re-assumed the role his father had assigned him in respect to Helena. *She* turned away her eyes and fixed them on the water, fascinated and absorbed. Had the idea of suicide really grazed her youthful brow with its invisible wing? Estacio went to her, grasped her hands, and urged her to come away. "Let us go in," he said for the third time. "Look, it's going to rain."

Helena allowed him to help her up; a shiver ran through her whole frame, and her hands, which he still held in his, were hot. "Come, you must rest," he continued. "You will get sick, and you have no right to; our love will never consent to it, never! Come, let us go . . ."

"Will you both love me, always?"

"Yes! Always!"

"It's impossible! There is a voice in the depth of your heart that will say to you, from time to time, this wretched word: 'adventuress!' "

"Helena!"

"I cannot be anything else in your eyes," she went on sadly. "Who will be able to convince you that your father's declaration was not obtained through my mother's cunning? Who will be able to give you proof that I, in yielding to my father's pleading, did nothing more than carry out a plan already in the making? There are doubts that are bound to poison your feeling toward me and make me suspect in your eyes. Another might endure it; I cannot face such a prospect!" She sank down on the bench, exhausted and breathless. Estacio spoke to her, with warmth and tenderness, his words pouring out in profusion: he swore that his family was incapable of the least suspicion, he begged her for his father's sake not to misjudge them. She smiled, but it was an incredulous smile.

Great drops of rain began to beat a tattoo on the trees. Estacio took Helena's hand to lead her to the house. She broke from him and went on a few steps ahead, where the rain fell with full force on her bare head and lightly clad body. When Estacio, beside himself with terror, hurried toward her, Helena ran from him but her feet could not outrun his nor would her strength, broken by so much emotional agitation, have permitted it. He overtook her, threw his arm around her waist and said, "What whim is this? Come, I want you to go inside with me."

At the touch of Estacio's arm, she trembled and made a movement as if to push him from her but her broken strength played traitor to her sense of shame. As she looked at him her eyes were those of a wounded doe, her knees gave way beneath her, and her weakened body would have sunk to the ground if Estacio's hands had not held her.

"Let me die!" she murmured.

"No!" he shouted. And with a swift gesture he lifted her limp body in his arms and started toward the house. The wind lashed them brutally; a sudden downpour of rain streamed over them in an immense sheet of water. Estacio kept going as fast as the weight of Helena's body permitted. Her head hung back toward the earth; her lips uttered disconnected, senseless phrases.

Dona Ursula saw this doleful spectacle entering the house and ran to take care of Helena, whom Estacio deposited on a sofa; from there she was carried to her bed. The fever which had begun before she went outside had now taken the poor girl into its custody. A doctor was summoned in haste. Father Melchior ran through the rain all the way to Estacio's house. The first hours were ones of anxiety and alarm; her condition was grave, said the doctor. Their loving hearts had already felt it so.

Dona Ursula now repaid the good offices Helena had lent her on a similar occasion—in spite of her years, which did not permit long vigils or constant stressful work. The good lady watched at the sick girl's bed all during that first night of uncertainty and terror. Mendonça had come to the house without suspecting anything wrong, for the illness they had told him Helena was suffering from he took to be of a temporary nature, and almost over; he received the sad news with a sinking heart.

For seven days the alternations in Helena's condition kept those who loved her hovering between confidence and despair. Some hours she was delirious and two names were constantly on her lips, Estacio's and her father's. In her hours of consciousness, she spoke little, uttered no name except Melchior's, for she wanted him constantly at her side. The chaplain obeyed, docilely. As he sat beside her, he saw her with sorrow but without desperation; first because he accepted without a murmur the decrees of the divine will, then because he was uncertain whether in such a situation life was better than death. In any case, he was a consolation to her.

On the fourth day, Camargo's family arrived home, and learning of Helena's illness hastened to Andarahy. On seeing Eugenia, Helena smiled sadly—a scintilla of envy that was immediately extinguished and died in her heart.

Estacio scarcely dared enter the sick girl's room, yet could not live away from it. His anguish was evident. He promised himself every kind of sacrifice in exchange for Helena's life, he watched for signs of hope in the doctor's face, sounded the hearts of his aunt and the priest. On the night of the seventh day after the scene in the garden, Dona Ursula, who was with Helena, sent in haste for her nephew and Father Melchior, who were in the next room. They ran to her. Helena had fainted but Dona Ursula thought she was dead. Coming to, the girl read her death warrant in their faces.

"Not yet," she murmured, "it is not yet death."

Dona Ursula drew near, kissed her, and spoke words of comfort.

"Just you see," Helena answered, "you'll see, I won't die. I'm only very ill."

Estacio tried to cheer her but his voice failed him at his first words, and he went out of the room. Melchior followed him.

"There is one thing that might perhaps save her," said the distressed youth, "that is, her father's presence. I am going to have a search made for him, everywhere. We are bound to find him; we must find him."

Melchior approved his idea, and did not mention that the remedy would perhaps come too late if it came at all. Estacio made arrangements for a search to begin the following morning. They returned to the sickroom. Helena had closed her eyes as if asleep. Then, between those four walls, there ensued a half hour of silence interrupted only by the movements the invalid made from time to time as if trying to change her position. At the end of that time she opened her eyes and whispered a few words. The doctor arrived, saw her, and told the family there was no hope.

While Melchior was giving precise orders for Helena to receive spiritual succor, Estacio went from the room, from the house, to get off where he could unburden his despair. He went down to the chácara, wandered over it, frantic, sobbing like a child, now hugging a tree, now kneeling, begging God for Helena's life. His heart was unacquainted with religious fervor but the spectre of death gave him what life had taken from him, and he prayed, alone, without hypocrisy or doubt. Mendonça came upon him in that final struggle between reality and hope. He did not offer him consolation; he had no consolation to give away because grief had also laid waste *his* heart. They wept in each other's arms for the loved woman who was even then slipping away from them.

A slave came to summon Estacio in haste. He climbed the stairs with unsteady feet, passed through the other rooms, entered Helena's room in a bewildered state, and fell on his knees beside her bed. Her eyes, already turned toward eternity, cast a last glance to earth and it was Estacio who received it — a look of love, yearning, and promise. Her pale, transparent hand groped for his head; he leaned over the bed's edge, hiding his tears, afraid to face the final moment. "Goodbye!" she whispered, and her soul burst its delicate earthly sheath, in its place only a dead body.

The night was cruel for them all. Dona Ursula, though profoundly overcome by grief and by her vigils, still would not consent that other hands shroud Helena; she alone paid her this last, sorrowful service. Death had not diminished her maiden beauty; on the contrary, the reflection of eternity seemed to give it a new, mysterious charm. Estacio contemplated her with wearied eyes. The priest's were moist; he had stood up under his grief until the moment of definite separation. Now that she was gone, he sank overcome beside those pale remains, the final spoils of generous illusions.

On the following day, when the procession was ready to leave, the women said their final adieux to the dead maiden. Dona Ursula was first, then followed Eugenia, then the others. Estacio watched them one by one mount the estrade on which the catafalque rested. Afterward, when they were about to close the coffin, he walked slowly toward it, climbed to the estrade, and for the last time gazed at that face, a little while ago so full of life, and at the wreath of *immortelles* around her head, in place of that other wreath, which he had a right to place there. Finally he too leaned over, and the dead girl's forehead received love's first kiss.

They closed the coffin. It seemed to him that it was he who was being shut inside it. The funeral procession left the house, Estacio sank into a chair, thinking of nothing, feeling nothing. Little by little the house was emptied of people; his friends had left; only one out of so many remained, mourning with him the bride so early promised, so early taken from him. He too finally left, only the family remaining, and their spiritual father, Melchior.

Alone with Estacio, the chaplain looked at him a long time, then lifted his eyes to the counselor's portrait, smiled a melancholy smile, turned back to Estacio, raised him, and embraced him with tender affection. "Courage, my son!" he said.

"All is ruined, Reverend Father, I have lost everything."

Meanwhile, at the house in Rio Comprido, Estacio's bride, horrified by Helena's death and depressed by the gloomy, somber ceremony, sadly retired to her bedroom. On the threshold she received her father's third kiss.

Designer: UC Press Staff
Compositor: Janet Sheila Brown
Printer: Vail-Ballou
Binder: Vail-Ballou
Text: Baskerville
Display: Gibson Roundhand